GREAT-TASTING LOW FAT RECIPES

Publications International, Ltd.

Louis Weber, C.E.O.
Publications International, Ltd.
7373 N. Cicero Ave.
Lincolnwood, IL 60646

Some of the products listed in this publication may be in limited distribution.

Front cover photography by Photo/Kevin Smith, Chicago.

Pictured on the front cover: Roast Beef and Pasta Salad *(page 20)*.

Pictured on the back cover: *(clockwise from top left):* Glazed Stuffed Pork Chop *(page 44)*, Mushrooms Rockefeller *(page 12)*, Fajita Salad *(page 32)* and Blueberry Angel Food Cake Roll *(page 90)*.

ISBN: 0-7853-1719-8

Manufactured in U.S.A.

8 7 6 5 4 3 2 1

Nutritional Analysis: Nutritional information is given for the recipes in this publication. Each analysis is based on the food items in the ingredient list, except ingredients labeled as "optional" or "for garnish." When more than one ingredient choice is listed, the first ingredient is used for analysis. If a range for the amount of an ingredient is given, the nutritional analysis is based on the lowest amount. Foods offered as "serve with" suggestions are not included in the analysis unless otherwise stated.

Microwave Cooking: Microwave ovens vary in wattage. The microwave cooking times given in this publication are approximate. Use the cooking times as guidelines and check for doneness before adding more time. Consult manufacturer's instructions for suitable microwave-safe cooking dishes.

GREAT-TASTING LOW FAT RECIPES

INTRODUCTION

Lower Fat for Healthier Living

Today, people everywhere are more aware about the importance of maintaining a healthful lifestyle. In addition to proper exercise, this includes eating foods lower in fat, sodium and cholesterol. It is widely known that most Americans' diets are too high in fat. A low fat diet reduces your risk of getting certain diseases and helps you maintain a healthy weight. Studies have shown that eating more than the recommended amount of fat (especially saturated fat) is associated with elevated blood cholesterol levels in some adults. High blood cholesterol levels are linked to an increased risk for heart disease. A high fat diet may also increase your chances for obesity and some types of cancer. Nutrition experts recommend diets that contain 30% or less of total daily calories from fat. The "30% calories from fat" goal applies to a total diet over time, not to a single food, serving of a recipe or meal.

About the Recipes

The American Heart Association has offered guidelines to help people adjust their diets in an effort to prevent heart and vascular diseases. The recipes that follow can help you make smart, healthy decisions about the foods you prepare. Every recipe is followed by a nutritional chart that tells you the number of calories, the grams (g) of fat, the milligrams (mg) of cholesterol and the milligrams (mg) of sodium for each serving of that recipe. To be considered for this magazine, recipes had to contain 30% or less calories from fat per serving. To find the approximate percentage of calories from fat use this easy 3-step process:

1. Multiply the grams of fat per serving by 9 (there are 9 calories in each gram of fat), to give you the number of calories from fat per serving.

2. Divide by the total number of calories per serving.

3. Multiply by 100%.

For example, imagine a 200 calorie sandwich that has 6

grams of fat. To find the percentage of calories from fat, first multiply the grams of fat by 9:

$$6 \times 9 = 54$$

Then, divide by the total number of calories in a serving:

$$54 \div 200 = .27$$

Multiply by 100% to get the percentage of calories from fat:

$$.27 \times 100\% = 27\%$$

Many of the recipes are low cholesterol and low sodium as well. These recipes contain less than 50 mg of cholesterol and less than 300 mg of sodium. As you browse through, you'll see that many of the recipes fall well below these numbers.

With more than 60 recipes contributed by America's largest food companies, you'll find plenty to choose from. There are appetizers, beverages, soups, breads, entrées, salads, vegetables, side dishes and desserts. From party fare to everyday meals, these wonderful low fat recipes are perfect to serve to family and friends.

About the Nutritional Information

The nutritional analysis of each recipe includes all the ingredients that are listed in that recipe, except ingredients labeled as "optional" or "for garnish." If a range is offered for an ingredient (1/8 to 1/4 teaspoon, for example) the first amount given was used to calculate the nutritional information. If an ingredient is presented with an option ("2 tablespoons margarine or butter"), the first item listed was used to calculate the nutritional information. Foods shown in photographs on the same serving plate and offered as "serve with" suggestions at the end of the recipe are not included in the recipe analysis unless it is stated in the per serving line.

The recipes in this magazine are NOT intended as a medically therapeutic program, nor as a substitute for medically approved diet plans for people on restricted diets. You should consult your physician before beginning any diet plan. The recipes offered here can be a part of a healthy lifestyle that meets recognized dietary guidelines. A healthy lifestyle includes not only eating a balanced diet, but engaging in proper exercise as well.

So discover a world of better living and great eating today with this taste-tempting collection of low fat recipes.

HEALTHY BEGINNINGS

FRUIT ANTIPASTO PLATTER

1 DOLE® Fresh Pineapple
2 medium, firm DOLE® Bananas, sliced diagonally
2 DOLE® Oranges, peeled and sliced
½ cup thinly sliced DOLE® Red Onion
½ pound low fat sharp Cheddar cheese, cut into 1-inch cubes
2 jars (6 ounces each) marinated artichoke hearts, drained and halved
DOLE® Green or Red Leaf Lettuce
½ cup fat free or light Italian salad dressing

• **Twist** crown from pineapple. Quarter pineapple lengthwise; remove core. Cut whole fruit from skin; slice fruit into thin wedges.

• **Arrange** fruit, onion, cheese and artichoke hearts on lettuce-lined platter; serve with dressing. Garnish, if desired.

Makes 10 servings

Nutrients per serving:	
Calories	195
Fat	4 g
Cholesterol	16 mg
Sodium	308 mg

WHITE SANGRIA

1 carton (64 ounces) DOLE® Pine-Orange-Guava Juice
2 cups fruity white wine
¼ cup orange-flavored liqueur
¼ cup sugar
1 DOLE® Orange, thinly sliced
1 lime, thinly sliced
2 cups sliced DOLE® Fresh Strawberries
Ice cubes
Mint sprigs for garnish

• **Combine** juice, wine, liqueur, sugar, orange, lime and strawberries in 2 large pitchers; cover and refrigerate 2 hours to blend flavors. Serve over ice. Garnish with mint sprigs.

Makes 20 servings

Nutrients per serving (4 ounces):	
Calories	93
Fat	trace
Cholesterol	0 mg
Sodium	7 mg

Fruit Antipasto Platter

Southwest Barbecue Kabobs

SOUTHWEST BARBECUE KABOBS

- **1 cup beer**
- **¾ cup A.1.® Steak Sauce**
- **2 cloves garlic, crushed**
- **2 teaspoons chili powder**
- **1 teaspoon ground cumin**
- **1½ pounds round steak, cut into ½-inch strips**
- **3 small red or green bell peppers, cut into 1-inch pieces**
- **1 teaspoon cornstarch**

In small bowl, combine beer, steak sauce, garlic, chili powder and cumin. Pour marinade over sliced steak in nonmetal dish. Cover; refrigerate 2 hours, stirring occasionally.

Remove steak from marinade; reserve marinade. Thread steak and pepper pieces alternately onto 6 skewers. In small saucepan, heat reserved marinade and cornstarch to a boil. Grill or broil kabobs, 4 inches from heat source, 15 minutes or until done, turning and brushing often with marinade. Heat remaining marinade to a boil; serve with kabobs.

Makes 6 appetizer servings

Nutrients per serving:	
Calories	198
Fat	4 g
Cholesterol	71 mg
Sodium	624 mg

BRUSCHETTA

- **2 Italian rolls (each 5 inches long)**
- **1¾ cups (14.5-ounce can) CONTADINA® Recipe Ready Diced Tomatoes, drained**
- **2 tablespoons chopped fresh basil**
- **1 tablespoon finely chopped onion**
- **1 tablespoon olive oil**
- **1 small clove garlic, crushed**
- **¼ teaspoon dried oregano leaves, crushed**
- **¼ teaspoon salt**
- **⅛ teaspoon ground black pepper**

Slice rolls in half lengthwise; toast. In small bowl, combine tomatoes, basil, onion, olive oil, garlic, oregano, salt and pepper. Spoon mixture onto toasted rolls. Broil 5 inches from heat source, until hot, about 2 minutes.

Makes 8 appetizer servings

Nutrients per serving:	
Calories	100
Fat	3 g
Cholesterol	17 mg
Sodium	280 mg

CRISPY BACON STICKS

- **½ cup (1½ ounces) grated Wisconsin Parmesan cheese, divided**
- **5 slices bacon, halved lengthwise**
- **10 breadsticks**

Microwave Directions: Spread ¼ cup cheese on plate. Press one side of bacon into cheese; wrap diagonally around breadstick with cheese-coated side toward stick. Place on paper plate or microwave-safe baking sheet lined with paper towels. Repeat with remaining bacon halves, cheese and breadsticks. Microwave on HIGH 4 to 6 minutes until bacon is cooked, checking for doneness after 4 minutes. Roll again in remaining ¼ cup Parmesan cheese. Serve warm.

Makes 10 sticks

Nutrients per serving (1 stick):	
Calories	150
Fat	4 g
Cholesterol	7 mg
Sodium	704 mg

Favorite recipe from **Wisconsin Milk Marketing Board**

LAHAINA SUNSET

2 fresh California peaches, halved
1 cup low fat milk
¼ cup pineapple juice
3 ice cubes, cracked
1 teaspoon rum extract

Place peaches, milk and pineapple juice in blender; process until smooth. Add ice and rum extract; process until smooth and frothy. Serve immediately.

Makes 3½ cups

Nutrients per serving (½ cup):

Calories	37
Fat	1 g
Cholesterol	3 mg
Sodium	18 mg

Favorite recipe from **California Tree Fruit Agreement**

MUSHROOMS ROCKEFELLER

18 large fresh button mushrooms (about 1 pound)
2 slices bacon
¼ cup chopped onion
1 package (10 ounces) frozen chopped spinach, thawed and squeezed dry
1 tablespoon lemon juice
1 teaspoon grated lemon peel
½ jar (2 ounces) chopped pimiento, drained
Lemon slices and lemon balm for garnish

1. Lightly oil 13×9-inch baking dish; set aside. Preheat oven to 375°F. Brush dirt from mushrooms; clean by wiping mushrooms with damp paper towel. Pull entire stem out of mushroom cap; set aside. Repeat with remaining mushrooms. Set caps aside.

2. Cut thin slice from base of each stem with paring knife; discard. Chop stems.

3. Cook bacon in medium skillet over medium heat until crisp. Remove bacon with tongs to paper towel; set aside. Add mushroom stems and onion to hot drippings in skillet. Cook and stir until onion is soft. Add spinach, lemon juice, lemon peel and pimiento; blend well. Stuff mushroom caps with spinach mixture using spoon; place in single layer in prepared baking dish. Crumble reserved bacon and sprinkle on top of mushrooms. Bake 15 minutes or until heated through. Garnish, if desired. Serve immediately.

Makes 18 appetizers

Nutrients per serving (1 appetizer):

Calories	17
Fat	trace
Cholesterol	trace
Sodium	26 mg

Mushrooms Rockefeller

ROASTED RED PEPPER DIP

1 envelope KNOX® Unflavored Gelatin
½ cup cold skim milk
1 cup skim milk, heated to boiling
1 container (8 ounces) 1% milkfat cottage cheese
¼ cup grated Parmesan cheese
½ teaspoon chopped garlic
½ teaspoon salt
⅛ teaspoon black pepper
1 jar (7 ounces) roasted red peppers, drained and chopped
1 cup loosely packed fresh basil leaves, chopped*
Suggested Dippers**

***Substitution:** Use 1 cup chopped fresh parsley plus 1 teaspoon dried basil.

****Suggested Dippers:** Use toasted French or Italian bread cubes, breadsticks or assorted cut-up vegetables.

In blender, sprinkle unflavored gelatin over cold milk; let stand 2 minutes. Add hot milk and process at low speed until gelatin is completely dissolved, about 2 minutes. Add cheeses, garlic, salt and black pepper; process at high speed until smooth, about 1 minute. Pour into 1-quart bowl; stir in red peppers and basil. Chill until set, about 3 hours. Beat with wire whisk or rotary beater until smooth. Serve with Suggested Dippers. *Makes 3 cups*

Nutrients per serving (1 tablespoon dip):	
Calories	10
Fat	0 g
Cholesterol	1 mg
Sodium	55 mg

BANANA–PINEAPPLE COLADA

½ ripe banana, peeled
½ cup fresh or canned pineapple chunks
½ cup pineapple juice
½ cup ice cubes
1 tablespoon sugar
¼ teaspoon coconut extract

Place all ingredients in blender or food processor; process until blended thoroughly. Serve immediately.

Makes 2 servings

Nutrients per serving:	
Calories	198
Fat	trace
Cholesterol	0 mg
Sodium	5 mg

Favorite recipe from **The Sugar Association, Inc.**

Left to Right: Banana-Pineapple Colada, Fruity Spritzer, Iced French Roast

ICED FRENCH ROAST

2 cups strong brewed French roast coffee, chilled
2 teaspoons sugar
½ teaspoon unsweetened cocoa powder
2 tablespoons low fat milk
Dash ground cinnamon

Place all ingredients in blender; process until combined. Pour over ice and serve immediately.

Makes 2 servings

Nutrients per serving:	
Calories	27
Fat	trace
Cholesterol	1 mg
Sodium	13 mg

Favorite recipe from **The Sugar Association, Inc.**

FRUITY SPRITZER

1 teaspoon strawberry extract
2 sugar cubes
1 cup chilled seltzer water

Place strawberry extract in small bowl; add sugar cubes and let stand 5 minutes. Place flavored sugar cubes in bottom of glass and add seltzer. Let cubes dissolve; serve immediately.

Makes 1 serving

Nutrients per serving:	
Calories	28
Fat	0 g
Cholesterol	0 mg
Sodium	3 mg

Favorite recipe from **The Sugar Association, Inc.**

Grilled Spiced Halibut, Pineapple and Pepper Skewers

2 tablespoons lemon juice or lime juice
1 teaspoon minced garlic
1 teaspoon chili powder
½ teaspoon ground cumin
¼ teaspoon ground cinnamon
⅛ teaspoon ground cloves
½ pound boneless skinless halibut steak, about 1 inch thick
½ small pineapple, peeled, halved lengthwise, cut into 24 pieces
1 large green or red bell pepper, cut into 24 squares

1. Combine lemon juice, garlic, chili powder, cumin, cinnamon and cloves in large resealable plastic food storage bag; knead until blended.

2. Rinse fish and pat dry. Cut into 12 cubes about 1 to 1¼ inches square. Add fish to bag; press out air and seal. Turn bag gently to coat fish with marinade. Refrigerate halibut 30 minutes to 1 hour. Soak 12 (6- to 8-inch) bamboo skewers in water while fish marinates.

3. Alternately thread 2 pieces pineapple, 2 pieces pepper and 1 piece fish onto each skewer.

4. Spray cold grid with nonstick cooking spray. Adjust grid 4 to 6 inches above heat. Preheat grill to medium-high heat. Place skewers on grill, cover if possible (or tent with foil) and grill 3 to 4 minutes or until grill marks appear on bottoms. Turn and grill skewers 3 to 4 minutes or until fish is opaque and flakes easily when tested with fork. *Makes 6 servings*

Nutrients per serving:

Calories	64
Fat	1 g
Cholesterol	12 mg
Sodium	23 mg

Hot Orchard Peach Cup

1 bottle (40 ounces) DOLE® Orchard Peach Juice
¼ cup packed brown sugar
2 cinnamon sticks
2 tablespoons margarine
½ cup peach schnapps (optional)
Additional cinnamon sticks for garnish (optional)

• **Combine** juice, brown sugar, 2 cinnamon sticks and margarine in Dutch oven. Heat to a boil. Remove from heat; discard cinnamon sticks. Add schnapps, if desired. Garnish with additional cinnamon sticks, if desired.
Makes 6 servings

Nutrients per serving (7 ounces):

Calories	181
Fat	4 g
Cholesterol	0 mg
Sodium	70 mg

Grilled Spiced Halibut, Pineapple and Pepper Skewers

ANTIPASTO MINI PIZZAS

- **1¾ cups (14.5-ounce can) CONTADINA® Pasta Ready Chunky Tomatoes**
- **¾ cup (4-ounce can) water-packed artichoke hearts, drained and coarsely chopped**
- **½ cup (2-ounce can) sliced ripe olives, drained**
- **½ cup chopped green bell pepper**
- **2 tablespoons grated Parmesan cheese**
- **8 plain bagels, lightly toasted, each half cut crosswise into 2 pieces**
- **1 cup (4 ounces) shredded mozzarella cheese**

In medium bowl, combine tomatoes, artichoke hearts, olives, bell pepper and Parmesan cheese. Place bagel pieces, cut-side up, on cookie sheets. Spoon about 1 tablespoon vegetable mixture onto each bagel piece. Sprinkle mozzarella cheese evenly over vegetable mixture. Bake in preheated 400°F oven 6 to 8 minutes or until heated through.

Makes 16 appetizer servings

Nutrients per serving:

Calories	140
Fat	3 g
Cholesterol	3 mg
Sodium	320 mg

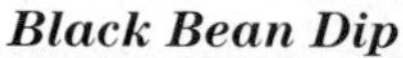

Black Bean Dip

BLACK BEAN DIP

1 can (15 ounces) black beans, rinsed, drained
½ cup MIRACLE WHIP® FREE® Nonfat Dressing
½ cup reduced-calorie sour cream
1 can (4 ounces) chopped green chilies, drained
2 tablespoons chopped cilantro
1 teaspoon chili powder
½ teaspoon garlic powder
Few drops hot pepper sauce

Mash beans with fork. Stir in dressing, sour cream, green chilies, cilantro, chili powder, garlic powder and hot pepper sauce until well blended; refrigerate. Serve with tortilla chips. *Makes 2¼ cups*

Prep Time: 10 minutes plus refrigerating

Nutrients per serving (2 tablespoons dip):	
Calories	70
Fat	1 g
Cholesterol	0 mg
Sodium	119 mg

PEACHES AND CREAM PUNCH

4 cups boiling water
6 LIPTON® Flo-Thru Regular or Decaffeinated Tea Bags
4 cans (12 ounces each) peach nectar, chilled
2 cups Champagne or seltzer, chilled
1 container (16 ounces) frozen vanilla lowfat yogurt

In teapot, pour boiling water over tea bags; cover and brew 5 minutes. Remove tea bags and cool.

In chilled 4-quart punch bowl, blend peach nectar with tea. Just before serving, add Champagne. Top with scoops of yogurt and garnish, if desired, with fresh peach slices. Serve immediately.
Makes 24 (4-ounce) servings

Nutrients per serving:	
Calories	77
Fat	0 g
Cholesterol	1 mg
Sodium	20 mg

SENSATIONAL SALADS

ROAST BEEF AND PASTA SALAD

9 ounces uncooked radiatore pasta
6 ounces lean roast beef
1 can (15 ounces) kidney beans, rinsed and drained
1 can (15 ounces) whole baby corn, rinsed and drained
1 can (10 ounces) diced tomatoes and green chilies
1 cup cherry tomato halves
½ cup sliced ripe olives (optional)
2 tablespoons minced fresh parsley
1 tablespoon minced fresh oregano
¼ cup olive oil

1. Cook pasta according to package directions, omitting salt; drain. Rinse in cold water; drain.

2. Slice beef into thin strips. Combine pasta, beef and remaining ingredients in large bowl. Toss to coat. Garnish with fresh oregano, if desired.

Makes 6 servings

Nutrients per serving:	
Calories	411
Fat	13 g
Cholesterol	23 mg
Sodium	576 mg

MEDITERRANEAN COUSCOUS

3 cups water
1 teaspoon salt
1 box (10 ounces) couscous
1 cup canned, rinsed and drained black beans
8 ounces cherry tomatoes, chopped
1 carrot, shredded
½ cup WISH-BONE® Fat Free Italian Dressing

In 2-quart saucepan, bring water and salt to a boil; stir in couscous. Cover, then remove from heat and let stand 5 minutes. Fluff with fork; set aside 10 minutes to cool. In large salad bowl, toss couscous with remaining ingredients; chill.

Makes about 6 (1-cup) servings

Nutrients per serving:	
Calories	172
Fat	trace
Cholesterol	0 mg
Sodium	587 mg

Roast Beef and Pasta Salad

CRUNCHY TUNA SALAD IN PEPPER BOATS

- **2 large green or yellow bell peppers, halved lengthwise, seeded**
- **½ cup MIRACLE WHIP® FREE® Dressing**
- **2 (6½-ounce) cans tuna in water, drained, flaked**
- **¼ cup chopped carrot**
- **¼ cup chopped celery**
- **¼ cup chopped red onion**
- **¼ cup chopped pecans (optional)**

Microwave Directions: Place pepper halves on plate. Microwave on HIGH (100% power) 1 minute; refrigerate.

Mix together remaining ingredients until well blended; refrigerate. Serve in pepper halves. *Makes 4 servings*

Prep Time: 20 minutes plus refrigerating
Microwave Cook Time: 1 minute

Nutrients per serving:	
Calories	170
Fat	2 g
Cholesterol	29 mg
Sodium	708 mg

Garden Chicken Salad

GARDEN CHICKEN SALAD

1¼ pounds skinless chicken breasts, cooked and cut up
½ cup chopped zucchini
¼ cup chopped carrot
2 tablespoons chopped onion
2 tablespoons chopped fresh parsley
⅓ cup nonfat mayonnaise dressing
¼ cup nonfat sour cream
½ teaspoon celery salt
⅛ teaspoon pepper
1 tablespoon CRISCO® Vegetable Oil
¼ cup sliced almonds
3 tomatoes, cut into wedges

1. Combine chicken, zucchini, carrot, onion and parsley in bowl.

2. Combine mayonnaise dressing, sour cream, celery salt and pepper in small bowl. Add to chicken mixture. Mix well. Cover. Refrigerate at least 2 hours.

3. Heat Crisco Oil in small skillet on medium heat. Add nuts. Cook and stir 4 minutes or until nuts are light golden brown. Drain on paper towels. Cool.

4. Serve salad on greens-covered plate, if desired. Surround with tomato wedges. Sprinkle with nuts. Garnish, if desired.

Makes 6 servings

Nutrients per serving:	
Calories	225
Fat	8 g
Cholesterol	75 mg
Sodium	365 mg

MEDITERRANEAN PASTA SALAD

1 package (8 ounces) refrigerated or frozen cheese tortellini
1 package (9 ounces) DOLE® Italian Style Vegetables
1 can (8 ounces) DOLE® Pineapple Chunks
2 tablespoons balsamic or red wine vinegar
1 tablespoon olive or vegetable oil
¼ pound fresh link turkey sausage, cooked, drained and sliced
1 medium DOLE® Red, Yellow or Green Bell Pepper, cut into 1-inch pieces

• **Prepare** tortellini as package directs, except add Italian style vegetables during last 2 minutes of cooking; reserve seasoning packet. Drain.

• **Drain** pineapple; reserve ¼ cup juice. Combine reserved juice, vinegar, oil and seasoning packet in large serving bowl.

• **Add** tortellini, vegetables, sausage, bell pepper and pineapple to dressing; toss to evenly coat. Serve at room temperature or chilled. Toss before serving. Garnish with fresh herbs, if desired.

Makes 6 servings

Nutrients per serving:	
Calories	184
Fat	5 g
Cholesterol	19 mg
Sodium	290 mg

Grilled Steak and Asparagus Salad

½ cup bottled light olive oil vinaigrette dressing
⅓ cup A.1.® Steak Sauce
1 (1-pound) beef top round steak
1 (10-ounce) package frozen asparagus spears, cooked and cooled
½ cup thinly sliced red bell pepper
8 large lettuce leaves
1 tablespoon toasted sesame seeds

In small bowl, blend vinaigrette and steak sauce. Pour marinade over steak in nonmetal dish. Cover; refrigerate 1 hour.

Remove steak from marinade. Grill or broil steak, 4 inches from heat source, 10 minutes or to desired doneness, basting occasionally with marinade and turning 2 or 3 times. Thinly slice steak; arrange steak, asparagus and red pepper on lettuce leaves. Heat marinade to a boil; pour over salad. Sprinkle with sesame seeds; serve immediately.

Makes 4 servings

Nutrients per serving:	
Calories	209
Fat	5 g
Cholesterol	65 mg
Sodium	857 mg

Chinese Chicken Salad

3 cups cooked rice, cooled
1½ cups cooked chicken breast cubes (about 1 whole breast)
1 cup sliced celery
1 can (8 ounces) sliced water chestnuts, drained
½ cup sliced fresh mushrooms
¼ cup sliced green onions
¼ cup chopped red bell pepper
¼ cup sliced black olives
2 tablespoons vegetable oil
2 tablespoons lemon juice
1 tablespoon soy sauce
½ teaspoon ground ginger
¼ to ½ teaspoon ground white pepper
Lettuce leaves

Combine rice, chicken, celery, water chestnuts, mushrooms, onions, bell pepper, and olives in large bowl. Place oil, lemon juice, soy sauce, ginger, and white pepper in small jar with lid; shake well. Pour over rice mixture. Toss lightly. Serve on lettuce leaves.

Makes 4 servings

Nutrients per serving:	
Calories	350
Fat	10 g
Cholesterol	41 mg
Sodium	644 mg

Favorite recipe from **USA Rice Council**

Grilled Steak and Asparagus Salad

Curried Salad Bombay

SESAME PORK SALAD

3 cups cooked rice
1½ cups slivered cooked pork*
¼ pound fresh snow peas, trimmed and julienned
1 medium cucumber, peeled, seeded, and julienned
1 medium red bell pepper, julienned
½ cup sliced green onions
2 tablespoons sesame seeds, toasted (optional)
¼ cup chicken broth
3 tablespoons rice or white wine vinegar
3 tablespoons soy sauce
1 tablespoon peanut oil
1 teaspoon sesame oil

*Substitute 1½ cups slivered cooked chicken for pork, if desired.

Combine rice, pork, snow peas, cucumber, bell pepper, onions, and sesame seeds in large bowl. Combine broth, vinegar, soy sauce, and oils in small jar with lid; shake well. Pour over rice mixture; toss lightly. Serve at room temperature or slightly chilled. *Makes 6 servings*

Nutrients per serving:	
Calories	269
Fat	8 g
Cholesterol	32 mg
Sodium	867 mg

Favorite recipe from **USA Rice Council**

CURRIED SALAD BOMBAY

1 package (1⅓ pounds) PERDUE® Fit 'n Easy® fresh skinless and boneless turkey breast
½ cup reduced-sodium chicken broth
½ cup reduced-calorie mayonnaise
½ cup plain low fat yogurt
1 tablespoon peach or mango chutney
2 to 3 teaspoons curry powder
Salt and ground black pepper to taste (optional)
1 red apple, unpeeled, cored and sliced
1 green apple, unpeeled, cored and sliced
¾ cup red and/or green seedless grapes
2 tablespoons snipped fresh chives
Curly green or Bibb lettuce

Microwave Directions: In deep 2-quart microwave-safe dish, place turkey breast and broth. Cover with plastic wrap and microwave at HIGH (100% power) 3 minutes. Reduce power to MEDIUM-HIGH (70% power) and microwave 7 minutes. Turn turkey breast over; cover with plastic wrap and microwave at MEDIUM-HIGH 7 minutes longer. Cover dish with aluminum foil and cool in broth.

In medium bowl, combine mayonnaise, yogurt, chutney, curry, salt and pepper; blend well. Remove turkey from broth and cut into small cubes; add to mayonnaise mixture. Add apples, grapes and chives; toss gently to coat ingredients with dressing. Serve salad on bed of lettuce.

Makes 6 servings

Nutrients per serving:	
Calories	241
Fat	8 g
Cholesterol	78 mg
Sodium	263 mg

LEMONY APPLE–BRAN SALAD

½ cup plain low-fat yogurt
1 tablespoon chopped parsley
1 teaspoon sugar
1 teaspoon lemon juice
½ teaspoon salt
2 cups chopped, cored red apples
½ cup thinly sliced celery
½ cup halved green grapes *or* ¼ cup raisins
½ cup KELLOGG'S® ALL-BRAN® Cereal

In medium bowl, combine yogurt, parsley, sugar, lemon juice and salt. Stir in apples, celery and grapes or raisins. Cover and refrigerate until ready to serve. Just before serving, stir in Kellogg's® All-Bran® cereal. Serve on lettuce, if desired.

Makes 6 servings

Nutrients per serving:	
Calories	60
Fat	1 g
Cholesterol	1 mg
Sodium	260 mg

MEXICAN SURIMI SALAD

- **12 ounces crab-flavored surimi seafood, chunks or salad-style, well flaked**
- **1 large tomato, halved, seeded and diced**
- **¼ cup sliced green onions**
- **¼ cup sliced black olives**
- **1 tablespoon chopped cilantro or fresh parsley**
- **¼ cup salsa**
- **3 cups salad greens, washed, drained and torn into bite-sized pieces**

Combine surimi seafood, tomato, green onions, olives and cilantro in medium bowl. Add salsa; toss gently to combine. Arrange salad greens onto 4 plates and divide seafood mixture onto greens.

Makes 4 servings

Nutrients per serving:	
Calories	122
Fat	3 g
Cholesterol	17 mg
Sodium	794 mg

Favorite recipe from **Surimi Seafood Education Center**

SMOKED TURKEY & FRUIT SALAD

- **1 package (16 ounces) DOLE® Classic Salad**
- **1 can (11 ounces) DOLE® Mandarin Oranges, drained**
- **4 ounces deli-sliced smoked turkey or chicken, cut into ½-inch slices**
- **½ cup DOLE® Seedless or Golden Raisins**
- **½ cup fat free or light ranch salad dressing**
- **1 can (20 ounces) DOLE® Pineapple Slices, drained and cut in half**

• **Toss** together salad, mandarin oranges, turkey and raisins in large bowl. Pour in dressing; toss to evenly coat.

• **Spoon** salad onto large serving platter. Arrange halved pineapple slices around salad.

Makes 4 servings

Prep Time: 15 minutes

Nutrients per serving:	
Calories	160
Fat	1 g
Cholesterol	8 mg
Sodium	413 mg

Smoked Turkey & Fruit Salad

Black and White Bean Salad

BLACK AND WHITE BEAN SALAD

½ cup MIRACLE WHIP® FREE® Nonfat Dressing
1 can (15 ounces) navy beans, drained and rinsed
1 can (15 ounces) black beans, drained and rinsed
½ cup green bell pepper strips
½ cup red onion slices
1 cucumber, chopped
3 tablespoons chopped fresh parsley
Dash black pepper

Mix together ingredients until well blended; refrigerate.

Makes 4 cups

Prep Time: 10 minutes

Nutrients per serving (½ cup):

Calories	200
Fat	1 g
Cholesterol	0 mg
Sodium	214 mg

ORIENTAL MANDARIN SALAD

SALAD

2 tablespoons peanut oil, divided
2 tablespoons light or regular soy sauce, divided
4 teaspoons sesame seeds, divided
½ teaspoon minced garlic, divided
¼ teaspoon ground ginger, divided
2 cups Rice CHEX® brand cereal
1 pound (16 ounces) boneless, skinless chicken breasts, cut into strips
6 cups torn spinach leaves
1 can (11 ounces) mandarin orange segments, drained
1 can (8 ounces) sliced water chestnuts, drained

DRESSING

¼ cup orange juice
1 tablespoon honey
1 teaspoon grated orange peel
1 teaspoon light or regular soy sauce

To make cereal croutons, in large skillet combine 1 tablespoon oil, 1 tablespoon soy sauce, 2 teaspoons sesame seeds, ¼ teaspoon garlic and ⅛ teaspoon ginger. Cook just until mixture comes to a boil, stirring occasionally. Add cereal, stirring until all pieces are evenly coated. Cook 2 minutes, stirring constantly. Spread on paper towels to cool.

In same skillet over high heat combine remaining 1 tablespoon oil, 1 tablespoon soy sauce, 2 teaspoons sesame seeds, ¼ teaspoon garlic and ⅛ teaspoon ginger. Add chicken, stirring until all pieces are evenly coated. Cook 3 to 4 minutes or until chicken is no longer pink, stirring constantly. Remove from heat. In large bowl combine chicken, spinach, orange segments and water chestnuts. In small bowl combine orange juice, honey, orange peel and 1 teaspoon soy sauce; toss with salad mixture. Add cereal croutons and toss. *Makes 4 servings*

Nutrients per serving:	
Calories	297
Fat	9 g
Cholesterol	64 mg
Sodium	423 mg

Fajita Salad

1 beef sirloin steak (6 ounces)
¼ cup fresh lime juice
2 tablespoons chopped fresh cilantro
1 clove garlic, minced
1 teaspoon chili powder
2 red bell peppers
1 medium onion
1 teaspoon olive oil
1 cup garbanzo beans, rinsed and drained
4 cups mixed salad greens
1 tomato, cut into wedges
1 cup salsa

1. Cut beef into 2×1×¼-inch strips. Place in resealable plastic food storage bag. Combine lime juice, cilantro, garlic and chili powder in small bowl. Pour over beef; seal bag. Let stand for 10 minutes, turning once.

2. Cut bell peppers into strips. Cut onion into slices. Heat olive oil in large nonstick skillet over medium-high heat until hot. Add bell peppers and onion. Cook and stir 6 minutes or until vegetables are crisp-tender. Remove from skillet. Add beef and marinade to skillet. Cook and stir 3 minutes or until meat is cooked through. Remove from heat. Add bell peppers, onion and garbanzo beans to skillet; toss to coat with pan juices. Cool slightly.

3. Divide salad greens evenly among serving plates. Top with beef mixture and tomato wedges. Serve with salsa. Garnish with sour cream and sprigs of cilantro, if desired. *Makes 4 servings*

Nutrients per serving:

Calories	160
Fat	5 g
Cholesterol	30 mg
Sodium	667 mg

Fajita Salad

Super Soups & Breads

Apple Sauce Irish Soda Bread

3 cups all-purpose flour
1 tablespoon sugar
2 teaspoons baking soda
1 teaspoon salt
1 cup low fat buttermilk
½ cup MOTT'S® Natural Apple Sauce
2 tablespoons margarine, melted
½ cup raisins
2 tablespoons skim milk

1. Preheat oven to 375°F. Spray 8-inch round baking pan with nonstick cooking spray.

2. In large bowl, combine flour, sugar, baking soda and salt.

3. In small bowl, combine buttermilk, apple sauce and margarine.

4. Add apple sauce mixture to flour mixture; stir until mixture forms a ball.

5. Turn out dough onto well-floured surface; knead raisins into dough. Pat into 7-inch round.

6. Place dough in prepared pan. Cut cross in top of dough, ¼ inch deep, with tip of sharp knife. Brush top of dough with milk.

7. Bake 35 minutes or until toothpick inserted in center comes out clean. Cool in pan 10 minutes. Invert onto wire rack; turn right side up. Cool completely. Cut into 16 wedges.

Makes 16 servings

Nutrients per serving:	
Calories	130
Fat	2 g
Cholesterol	0 mg
Sodium	270 mg

Apple Sauce Irish Soda Bread

EASY CHILI CON CARNE

½ medium onion, chopped
1 stalk celery, sliced
1 teaspoon chili powder
1 can (15¼ ounces) kidney beans, drained
1 can (14½ ounces) DEL MONTE® Chili Style Chunky Tomatoes
1 cup cooked cubed beef

Microwave Directions: In 2-quart microwavable dish, combine first 3 ingredients. Add 1 tablespoon water. Cover; microwave on HIGH 3 to 4 minutes. Add remaining ingredients. Cover; microwave on HIGH 6 to 8 minutes or until heated, stirring halfway through cooking time. For a spicier chili, serve with hot pepper sauce.

Makes 4 servings

Prep Time: 8 minutes
Microwave Cook Time: 12 minutes

Nutrients per serving:	
Calories	193
Fat	3 g
Cholesterol	28 mg
Sodium	612 mg

CORN BREAD

1 cup all-purpose flour
1 cup yellow cornmeal
¼ cup sugar
1 tablespoon baking powder
1 teaspoon salt
1 cup skim milk
4 egg whites
¼ cup MOTT'S® Natural Apple Sauce

1. Preheat oven to 400°F. Spray 8-inch square baking pan with nonstick cooking spray.

2. In large bowl, combine flour, cornmeal, sugar, baking powder and salt.

3. In small bowl, combine milk, egg whites and apple sauce.

4. Stir apple sauce mixture into flour mixture just until moistened. Spread batter into prepared pan.

5. Bake 20 to 25 minutes or until toothpick inserted in center comes out clean. Cut into 9 squares; serve warm.

Makes 9 servings

Nutrients per serving:	
Calories	150
Fat	1 g
Cholesterol	0 mg
Sodium	370 mg

BRAN AND HONEY RYE BREADSTICKS

1 package (¼ ounce) active dry yeast
1 teaspoon sugar
1½ cups warm water (110°F)
3¾ cups all-purpose flour, divided
1 tablespoon honey
1 tablespoon vegetable oil
½ teaspoon salt
1 cup rye flour
½ cup whole bran cereal
Skim milk

1. Dissolve yeast and sugar in warm water in large bowl. Let stand 10 minutes. Add 1 cup all-purpose flour, honey, oil and salt. Beat with electric mixer at

Bran and Honey Rye Breadsticks

medium speed 3 minutes. Stir in rye flour, bran cereal and additional 2 cups all-purpose flour or enough to make moderately stiff dough.

2. Knead dough on lightly floured surface 10 minutes or until smooth and elastic, adding remaining ¾ cup all-purpose flour as necessary to prevent sticking. Place in greased bowl; turn over to grease surface. Cover with damp cloth; let rise in warm place 40 to 45 minutes or until doubled in bulk.

3. Spray 2 baking sheets with nonstick cooking spray. Punch dough down. Divide into 24 equal pieces on lightly floured surface. Roll each piece into an 8-inch rope. Place on prepared baking sheets. Cover with damp cloth; let rise in warm place 30 to 35 minutes or until doubled in bulk.

4. Preheat oven to 375°F. Brush breadsticks with milk. Bake 18 to 20 minutes or until breadsticks are golden brown. Remove from baking sheets. Cool on wire racks.

Makes 24 breadsticks

Nutrients per serving (2 breadsticks):

Calories	198
Fat	2 g
Cholesterol	0 mg
Sodium	109 mg

CHEESY HOT PEPPER BREAD

3 cups KELLOGG'S® NUTRI–GRAIN® Wheat Cereal, crushed to fine crumbs
5 to 6 cups all-purpose flour, divided
2 packages active dry yeast
2 teaspoons salt
1½ cups low-fat milk
¼ cup vegetable oil
2 eggs
1½ cups (6 ounces) shredded Monterey Jack cheese with jalapeño peppers
½ cup finely chopped onions
2 tablespoons margarine, melted (optional)

In large electric mixer bowl, stir together crushed Kellogg's® Nutri-Grain® cereal, 2 cups flour, yeast and salt. Set aside.

Heat milk and oil until very warm (120° to 130°F). Gradually add to cereal mixture and beat until well combined. Add eggs. Beat on medium speed for 2 minutes. Stir in cheese and onions.

By hand, stir in enough remaining flour to make a stiff dough. On well-floured surface, knead dough about 5 minutes or until smooth and elastic. Place dough in lightly greased bowl, turning once to grease top. Cover loosely. Let rise in warm place (80° to 85°F) until double in volume (about 1 hour).

Punch dough down. Divide into 4 pieces. On lightly floured surface, roll each into a 7×10-inch rectangle. Roll up loaves from long sides. Place, seam-sides-down, on greased baking sheets. Let rise in warm place until double in volume. Make diagonal slits across tops of loaves.

Bake at 400°F about 15 minutes or until golden brown. Brush baked loaves with margarine, if desired. Serve warm or cool.

Makes 4 loaves, 12 slices per loaf

Nutrients per serving:	
Calories	100
Fat	3 g
Cholesterol	10 mg
Sodium	129 mg

GOLDEN TOMATO SOUP

4 teaspoons reduced-calorie margarine
1 cup chopped onion
2 cloves garlic, coarsely chopped
½ cup chopped carrot
¼ cup chopped celery
8 medium tomatoes, blanched, peeled, seeded and chopped
6 cups chicken broth
¼ cup uncooked rice
2 tablespoons tomato paste
1 tablespoon Worcestershire sauce
½ teaspoon dried thyme leaves, crushed
¼ to ½ teaspoon ground black pepper
5 drops hot pepper sauce

Melt margarine in large Dutch oven over medium-high heat. Add onion and garlic; cook and stir 1 to 2 minutes or until onion is tender. Add carrot and celery; cook and stir 7 to 9 minutes or until tender, stirring frequently. Stir in tomatoes, broth, rice, tomato paste, Worcestershire sauce, thyme, black pepper and hot pepper sauce. Reduce heat to low; cook about 30 minutes, stirring frequently.

Remove from heat. Let cool about 10 minutes. In food processor or blender, process soup in small batches until smooth. Return soup to Dutch oven; simmer 3 to 5 minutes or until heated through. Garnish as desired.

Makes 8 servings

Nutrients per serving:	
Calories	91
Fat	2 g
Cholesterol	1 mg
Sodium	641 mg

Favorite recipe from **Florida Tomato Committee**

Golden Tomato Soup

WHOLE WHEAT HERB BREAD

⅔ cup water
⅔ cup skim milk
2 teaspoons sugar
2 envelopes active dry yeast
3 egg whites, lightly beaten
3 tablespoons olive oil
1 teaspoon salt
½ teaspoon dried basil leaves
½ teaspoon dried oregano leaves
4 to 4½ cups whole wheat flour

1. Bring water to a boil in small saucepan. Remove from heat; stir in milk and sugar. When mixture is warm (110° to 115°F), add yeast. Mix well; let stand 10 minutes or until bubbly.

2. Combine egg whites, oil, salt, basil and oregano in large bowl until well blended. Add yeast mixture; mix well. Add 4 cups flour, ½ cup at a time, mixing well after each addition, until dough is no longer sticky. Knead about 5 minutes or until smooth and elastic, adding more flour if dough is sticky. Form into a ball. Cover and let rise in warm place about 1 hour or until doubled in bulk.

3. Preheat oven to 350°F. Punch dough down and place on lightly floured surface. Divide into 4 pieces and roll each piece into a ball. Lightly spray baking sheet with nonstick cooking spray. Place dough balls on prepared baking sheet. Bake 30 to 35 minutes or until golden brown and loaves sound hollow when tapped with finger. *Makes 24 slices*

Nutrients per serving:

Calories	99
Fat	2 g
Cholesterol	<1 mg
Sodium	101 mg

GAZPACHO

2 carrots, peeled
1 cucumber, unpeeled
1 medium tomato
½ red bell pepper, seeded
2 cups spicy tomato juice
½ cup water
½ cup tomato sauce
¼ cup chopped scallions
3 tablespoons vinegar
2 teaspoons sugar
1 clove garlic, minced
1 can (15 ounces) navy beans, drained and rinsed

Cut carrots, cucumber, tomato and pepper into large chunks. Add tomato juice, water, tomato sauce, scallions, vinegar, sugar and garlic. Place in food processor or blender; process to make chunky purée. Pour into large serving bowl; stir in beans. Cover and refrigerate until chilled. Serve cold. *Makes 6 servings*

Nutrients per serving:

Calories	92
Fat	trace
Cholesterol	0 mg
Sodium	310 mg

Favorite recipe from **The Sugar Association, Inc.**

Whole Wheat Herb Bread

Cheesy Onion Flatbread

POTATO–CHEESE CALICO SOUP

1 pound potatoes, peeled and thinly sliced
1 cup sliced onion
2½ cups chicken broth
½ cup low-fat milk
1 cup sliced mushrooms
½ cup diced red bell pepper
½ cup sliced green onions
1 cup (4 ounces) finely shredded Wisconsin Asiago Cheese
Salt and black pepper (optional)
2 tablespoons chopped fresh parsley

In 3-quart saucepan, combine potatoes, 1 cup onion and broth. Bring to a boil. Reduce heat to low. Cover; cook until potatoes are tender, about 10 minutes. Transfer to blender container; blend until smooth. Return to saucepan. Stir in milk, mushrooms, bell pepper and green onions. Bring to a simmer over medium-low heat. Add cheese, a few tablespoons at a time, stirring to melt. Season with salt and black pepper. Sprinkle with parsley.

Makes 6 servings, 6 cups

Nutrients per serving (1 cup):

Calories	151
Fat	4 g
Cholesterol	9 mg
Sodium	526 mg

Favorite recipe from **Wisconsin Milk Marketing Board**

CHEESY ONION FLATBREAD

½ cup plus 3 tablespoons honey, divided
2⅓ cups warm water (105° to 115°F), divided
1½ packages active dry yeast
6 tablespoons olive oil, divided
3 cups whole wheat flour
⅓ cup cornmeal
4½ teaspoons coarse salt
3 to 4 cups all-purpose flour, divided
1 large red onion, thinly sliced
1 cup red wine vinegar
Additional cornmeal
1 cup grated Parmesan cheese
½ teaspoon onion salt
Freshly ground black pepper to taste

1. Place 3 tablespoons honey in large bowl. Pour ⅓ cup water over honey. Do not stir. Sprinkle yeast over water. Let stand about 15 minutes until bubbly. Add remaining 2 cups water, 3 tablespoons olive oil, whole wheat flour and cornmeal. Mix until well blended. Stir in salt and 2 cups all-purpose flour. Gradually stir in enough remaining flour until mixture clings to side of bowl.

2. Turn dough out onto lightly floured surface. Knead in enough remaining flour to make a smooth and satiny dough, about 10 minutes. Divide dough in half. Place each half in large, lightly greased bowl; turn over to grease surface. Cover; let rise in warm place (80° to 85°F) until doubled.

3. Meanwhile, combine onion, vinegar and remaining ½ cup honey. Marinate at room temperature at least 1 hour.

4. Grease two 12-inch pizza pans; sprinkle each with additional cornmeal. Stretch dough and pat into pans; create valleys with fingertips. Cover; let rise in warm place until doubled, about 1 hour.

5. Preheat oven to 400°F. Drain onion; scatter over dough. Sprinkle with remaining 3 tablespoons olive oil, cheese and onion salt. Season with pepper.

6. Bake 25 to 30 minutes or until flatbread is crusty and golden. Cut each flatbread into 8 wedges. Serve warm.

Makes 2 flatbreads, 8 wedges each

Nutrients per serving (1 wedge):

Calories	296
Fat	8 g
Cholesterol	5 mg
Sodium	916 mg

MAIN EVENTS

GLAZED STUFFED PORK CHOPS

2 medium cooking apples
3 cups prepared cabbage slaw blend
¼ cup raisins
¾ cup apple cider, divided
2 tablespoons maple-flavored pancake syrup
4 teaspoons spicy brown mustard, divided
2 lean pork chops, 1 inch thick (about 6 ounces each)
Nonstick cooking spray
2 teaspoons cornstarch

1. Quarter and core apples. Chop 6 quarters; reserve remaining 2 quarters. Combine chopped apples, slaw blend, raisins, ¼ cup apple cider, syrup and 2 teaspoons mustard in large saucepan. Cover and cook over medium heat 5 minutes or until cabbage is tender.

2. Make a pocket in each pork chop by cutting horizontally through chop almost to bone. Fill each pocket with about ¼ cup cabbage-apple mixture. Keep remaining cabbage-apple mixture warm over low heat.

3. Spray medium nonstick skillet with cooking spray; heat over medium heat until hot. Brown pork chops about 3 minutes on each side. Add ¼ cup apple cider. Reduce heat to low; cover and cook 8 minutes or until pork is barely pink in center. Remove pork from skillet; keep warm.

4. Add liquid from remaining cabbage-apple mixture to skillet. Combine remaining ¼ cup cider, 2 teaspoons mustard and cornstarch in small bowl until smooth. Stir into liquid in skillet. Simmer over medium heat until thickened. Spoon glaze over chops and cabbage-apple mixture. Slice remaining 2 apple quarters; divide between servings.

Makes 2 servings

Nutrients per serving:	
Calories	490
Fat	12 g
Cholesterol	53 mg
Sodium	227 mg

Glazed Stuffed Pork Chops

BAJA FISH AND RICE BAKE

3 tablespoons vegetable oil
¾ cup chopped onion
½ cup chopped celery
1 clove garlic, minced
½ cup uncooked medium grain white rice
3½ cups (two 14.5-ounce cans) CONTADINA® Stewed Tomatoes, cut up, undrained
1 teaspoon lemon pepper seasoning
½ teaspoon salt
⅛ teaspoon cayenne pepper
1 pound fish fillets (any firm white fish)
¼ cup finely chopped fresh parsley
Lemon slices (optional)

Heat oil in large skillet over medium heat; sauté onion, celery and garlic. Stir in rice; sauté about 5 minutes, or until rice browns slightly. Add tomatoes and juice, lemon pepper, salt and cayenne pepper. Place fish fillets in bottom of 12×7½×2-inch baking dish. Spoon rice mixture over fish. Cover with foil; bake in preheated 400°F oven for 45 to 50 minutes or until rice is tender. Allow to stand 5 minutes before serving. Sprinkle with parsley. Garnish with lemon slices, if desired.

Makes 6 servings

Microwave Directions: Combine onion, celery and garlic in microwave-safe bowl. Microwave at HIGH power (100%) for 3 minutes. Stir in rice, tomatoes and juice, lemon pepper, salt and cayenne pepper. Microwave at HIGH power for an additional 5 minutes. Place fish fillets in

Baja Fish and Rice Bake

12×7½×2-inch microwave-safe baking dish. Spoon tomato mixture over fish. Cover tightly with plastic wrap, turning up corner to vent. Microwave at HIGH power for 20 to 25 minutes or until rice is tender. Allow to stand 5 minutes before serving. Serve as above.

Nutrients per serving:	
Calories	241
Fat	8 g
Cholesterol	38 mg
Sodium	580 mg

Mediterranean Meatballs and Couscous

1 can (about 14 ounces) defatted ⅓-less-salt chicken broth
2½ cups water
1½ cups precooked couscous*
¾ cup golden raisins
¼ cup chopped parsley
3 tablespoons lemon juice, divided
3 teaspoons grated lemon peel, divided
2 teaspoons ground cinnamon, divided
1 teaspoon turmeric
½ teaspoon ground cumin
1 pound ground round beef
½ cup crushed saltine crackers
¼ cup evaporated skimmed milk
½ teaspoon dried oregano leaves

*Package label may not indicate couscous is precooked. Check ingredient list for "precooked semolina."

1. Pour chicken broth and water into 2-quart saucepan. Bring to a boil over high heat. Remove from heat. Add couscous, raisins, parsley, 2 tablespoons lemon juice, 2 teaspoons lemon peel, 1½ teaspoons cinnamon, turmeric and cumin. Cover and let stand 5 minutes.

2. Combine beef, crackers, milk, remaining 1 tablespoon lemon juice, 1 teaspoon lemon peel, ½ teaspoon cinnamon and oregano in large bowl. Mix until well blended. Shape into 24 meatballs. Place in large microwavable baking dish. Cover loosely with waxed paper. Microwave at HIGH 4 minutes or until meatballs are cooked through.

3. Stir couscous mixture and spoon onto serving platter. Arrange meatballs on couscous. Garnish with lemon wedges and fresh oregano, if desired.

Makes 6 servings

Nutrients per serving:	
Calories	434
Fat	11 g
Cholesterol	50 mg
Sodium	180 mg

MICROWAVED LEMON–APPLE FISH ROLLS

4 sole, cod or red snapper fillets (1 pound)
Grated peel of 1 SUNKIST® Lemon, divided
1 teaspoon dried dill weed, divided
¾ cup plus 2 tablespoons apple juice, divided
Juice of ½ SUNKIST® Lemon
2 tablespoons finely minced onion
1 tablespoon unsalted margarine
1 tablespoon all-purpose flour
1 tablespoon chopped parsley

Sprinkle fish with half the lemon peel and half the dill. Roll up each fillet; place, seam-side-down, in 8-inch round microwavable dish. Combine ¾ cup apple juice, lemon juice, onion, remaining lemon peel and dill; pour over fish. Dot with margarine. Cover with vented plastic wrap. Microwave at HIGH 3 minutes. Uncover; spoon cooking liquid over fish. Cook, covered, 3 to 4 minutes or until fish flakes easily with fork. Let stand, covered, while making sauce.

Pour cooking liquid from fish into small microwavable bowl. Blend remaining 2 tablespoons apple juice into flour; stir into cooking liquid. Microwave at HIGH 3 to 4 minutes; stir twice until sauce boils and slightly thickens. Add parsley; spoon over fish.

Makes 4 servings

Nutrients per serving:

Calories	164
Fat	4 g
Cholesterol	55 mg
Sodium	94 mg

BEEF & BEAN BURRITOS

Nonstick cooking spray
½ pound beef round steak, cut into ½-inch pieces
3 cloves garlic, minced
1 can (about 15 ounces) pinto beans, rinsed and drained
1 can (4 ounces) diced mild green chilies, drained
¼ cup finely chopped fresh cilantro
6 (6-inch) flour tortillas
½ cup (2 ounces) shredded reduced fat Cheddar cheese

1. Spray nonstick skillet with cooking spray; heat over medium heat until hot. Add steak and garlic; cook and stir 5 minutes or until steak is cooked to desired doneness. Stir beans, chilies and cilantro into skillet; cook and stir 5 minutes or until heated through.

2. Spoon steak mixture evenly down center of each tortilla; sprinkle with cheese. Fold bottom end of tortilla over filling; roll to enclose. Garnish, if desired.

Makes 6 servings

Nutrients per serving:

Calories	278
Fat	7 g
Cholesterol	31 mg
Sodium	956 mg

Beef & Bean Burritos

Chicken Phyllo Wraps

Vegetable cooking spray
1 pound ground chicken
1 cup chopped fresh mushrooms
1 medium onion, chopped
3 cups cooked rice (cooked without salt and fat)
1 cup nonfat low-salt ricotta cheese
1 package (10 ounces) chopped spinach, thawed and well drained
1 can (2¼ ounces) sliced black olives, drained
¼ cup pine nuts, toasted*
2 cloves garlic, minced
1 teaspoon ground oregano
1 teaspoon lemon pepper
12 phyllo dough sheets

*To toast nuts, place on baking sheet. Bake at 350°F 5 to 7 minutes or until lightly browned.

Coat large skillet with cooking spray; heat over medium-high heat until hot. Add chicken, mushrooms, and onion; cook and stir 2 to 4 minutes or until chicken is no longer pink and vegetables are tender. Reduce heat to medium. Add rice, ricotta cheese, spinach, olives, nuts, garlic, oregano, and lemon pepper; cook and stir 3 to 4 minutes until well blended and thoroughly heated. Working with 1 phyllo sheet at a time, spray 1 sheet with cooking spray; fold sheet in half lengthwise. Place ¾ to 1 cup rice mixture on one end of phyllo strip. Fold left bottom corner over mixture, forming a triangle. Continue folding back and forth into triangle at end of strip. Repeat with remaining phyllo sheets and rice mixture. Place triangles, seam sides down, on baking sheets coated with cooking spray. Coat top of each triangle with cooking spray. Bake at 400°F 15 to 20 minutes or until golden brown. Serve immediately.

Makes 12 servings

Nutrients per serving:

Calories	219
Fat	6 g
Cholesterol	27 mg
Sodium	224 mg

Favorite recipe from **USA Rice Council**

Chicken Phyllo Wraps

FISH FRANÇOISE

1 can (14½ ounces) DEL MONTE® Original Recipe Stewed Tomatoes
1 tablespoon lemon juice
2 cloves garlic, minced
½ teaspoon dried tarragon leaves, crushed
⅛ teaspoon black pepper
3 tablespoons whipping cream
Vegetable oil
1½ pounds firm white fish (such as halibut or cod)
Lemon wedges

Preheat broiler; position rack 4 inches from heat. In large saucepan, combine tomatoes with liquid, lemon juice, garlic, tarragon and pepper. Cook, uncovered, over medium-high heat about 10 minutes or until liquid has evaporated. Add cream. Cook over low heat 5 minutes or until very thick; set aside. Brush broiler pan with oil. Arrange fish on pan; season with salt and pepper, if desired. Broil fish 3 to 4 minutes per side or until fish flakes easily with fork. Spread tomato mixture over top of fish. Broil 1 minute. Serve immediately with lemon wedges.

Makes 4 servings

Prep Time: 5 minutes
Cook Time: 19 minutes

Nutrients per serving:

Calories	240
Fat	7 g
Cholesterol	78 mg
Sodium	341 mg

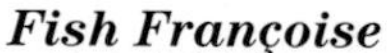

Fish Françoise

APPLESAUCE–STUFFED TENDERLOIN

2 pork tenderloins (about 1 pound each), trimmed
¼ cup dry vermouth or apple juice
⅔ cup chunky applesauce
¼ cup finely chopped dry-roasted peanuts
¼ teaspoon salt
¼ teaspoon finely crushed fennel seeds
⅛ teaspoon black pepper

Using sharp knife, form a "pocket" in each pork tenderloin by cutting a lengthwise slit down center almost to, but not through, bottom of each. Place in nonmetal dish. Pour vermouth in pockets and over tenderloins; cover. Marinate about 1 hour at room temperature.

Heat oven to 375°F. Spray 15×10-inch jelly-roll pan or shallow baking pan with nonstick cooking spray. In small bowl, combine remaining ingredients; blend. Spoon mixture into pockets. Secure pockets with toothpicks. Place stuffed tenderloins in prepared pan. Roast about 30 minutes, or until meat thermometer registers 155°F. Let stand 5 to 10 minutes before slicing. *Makes 8 servings*

Nutrients per serving:

Calories	179
Fat	6 g
Cholesterol	79 mg
Sodium	131 mg

Favorite recipe from **National Pork Producers Council**

KUNG PAO CHICKEN

1 pound boneless, skinless chicken breasts, cut into 1-inch pieces
1 tablespoon cornstarch
2 teaspoons CRISCO® Vegetable Oil
3 tablespoons chopped green onions with tops
2 cloves garlic, minced
¼ to 1½ teaspoons crushed red pepper
¼ to ½ teaspoon ground ginger
2 tablespoons wine vinegar
2 tablespoons soy sauce
2 teaspoons sugar
⅓ cup unsalted dry roasted peanuts
4 cups hot cooked rice (cooked without salt or fat)

1. Combine chicken and cornstarch in small bowl; toss. Heat Crisco Oil in large skillet or wok on medium-high heat. Add chicken. Stir-fry 5 to 7 minutes or until no longer pink in center. Remove from skillet. Add onions, garlic, red pepper and ginger to skillet. Stir-fry 15 seconds. Remove from heat.

2. Combine vinegar, soy sauce and sugar in small bowl. Stir well. Add to skillet. Return chicken to skillet. Stir until coated. Stir in nuts. Heat thoroughly, stirring occasionally. Serve over hot rice. *Makes 4 servings*

Nutrients per serving (one-fourth of recipe):

Calories	500
Fat	10 g
Cholesterol	65 mg
Sodium	595 mg

Louisiana Jambalaya

LIGHT CHICKEN CORDON BLEU

½ cup seasoned dry bread crumbs
1 tablespoon grated Parmesan cheese
1 teaspoon chopped fresh parsley
½ teaspoon paprika
1 package (1 pound) PERDUE® Fit 'n Easy® fresh skinless and boneless Oven Stuffer Roaster thin-sliced breast
1 package (6 ounces) reduced-fat Swiss cheese slices
1 package (6 ounces) turkey ham slices
1 egg white, beaten

Microwave Directions: In shallow bowl, combine first four ingredients. On each chicken breast slice, place 1 slice Swiss cheese and 2 overlapping slices ham; roll up, jelly-roll style, and secure with toothpick. Dip rolls in egg white, then coat with bread crumb mixture. In microwavable dish, arrange chicken rolls, seam sides down, in circular pattern. Cover with waxed paper; microwave at MEDIUM-HIGH (70% power) 5 minutes. Rearrange rolls; cover with double thickness of paper towels. Microwave at MEDIUM-HIGH 8 minutes. Let stand, uncovered, 5 to 10 minutes.

Makes 5 servings

Nutrients per serving:	
Calories	269
Fat	8 g
Cholesterol	91 mg
Sodium	676 mg

LOUISIANA JAMBALAYA

1½ pounds chicken tenders
½ teaspoon salt
½ teaspoon ground black pepper
1 tablespoon vegetable oil
¾ pound smoked turkey sausage, cut into ¼-inch slices
2 medium onions, chopped
1 large green bell pepper, chopped
1 cup chopped celery
1 clove garlic, minced
2 cups uncooked long grain white rice (not converted)
¼ to ½ teaspoon ground red pepper
2½ cups chicken broth
1 cup sliced green onions
1 medium tomato, chopped
Celery leaves for garnish

Season chicken with salt and black pepper. Heat oil in large saucepan or Dutch oven over high heat until hot. Add chicken, stirring until brown on all sides. Add sausage; cook 2 to 3 minutes. Remove chicken and sausage from saucepan; set aside. Add chopped onions, green pepper, celery, and garlic to same saucepan; cook and stir over medium-high heat until crisp-tender. Stir in rice, red pepper, broth, and reserved chicken and sausage; bring to a boil. Reduce heat to low; cover and simmer 30 minutes. Stir in green onions and tomato. Garnish with celery leaves. Serve immediately.

Makes 8 servings

Microwave Directions: Season chicken with salt and black pepper. Place oil in deep 3-quart microproof baking dish. Add chicken; cover with wax paper and cook on HIGH 3 minutes, stirring after 2 minutes. Add sausage; cover with wax paper and cook on HIGH 1 minute. Remove chicken and sausage with slotted spoon; set aside. Add chopped onions, green pepper, celery, and garlic to same dish. Cover and cook on HIGH 4 minutes, stirring after 2 minutes. Stir in rice, red pepper, broth, and reserved chicken and sausage; cover and cook on HIGH 8 minutes or until boiling. Reduce setting to MEDIUM (50% power); cover and cook 30 minutes, stirring after 15 minutes. Stir in green onions and tomato. Let stand 5 minutes before serving. Garnish with celery leaves.

Nutrients per serving:	
Calories	403
Fat	10 g
Cholesterol	79 mg
Sodium	739 mg

Favorite recipe from **USA Rice Council**

GRILLED VEGETABLE KABOBS

1 large red or green bell pepper
1 large zucchini
1 large yellow squash or additional zucchini
12 ounces large mushrooms
2 tablespoons olive oil
2 tablespoons red wine vinegar
1 package (7.2 ounces) RICE-A-RONI® Herb & Butter
1 large tomato, chopped
¼ cup grated Parmesan cheese

1. Cut red pepper into twelve 1-inch pieces. Cut zucchini and yellow squash crosswise into twelve ½-inch slices. Marinate red pepper, zucchini, yellow squash and mushrooms in combined oil and vinegar 15 minutes.

2. Alternately thread marinated vegetables onto 4 large skewers. Brush with any remaining oil mixture; set aside.

3. Prepare Rice-A-Roni Mix as package directs.

4. While Rice-A-Roni is simmering, grill kabobs over medium-low coals or broil 4 to 5 inches from heat 12 to 14 minutes or until tender and browned, turning once.

5. Stir tomato into rice. Serve rice topped with kabobs. Sprinkle with cheese. *Makes 4 servings*

Nutrients per serving:

Calories	320
Fat	10 g
Cholesterol	5 mg
Sodium	1200 mg

BEEF 'N' BROCCOLI

½ cup A.1.® Steak Sauce
¼ cup soy sauce
2 cloves garlic, crushed
1 pound top round steak, thinly sliced
1 (16-ounce) bag frozen broccoli, red bell peppers, bamboo shoots and mushrooms, thawed*
Hot cooked rice (optional)

*1 (16-ounce) bag frozen broccoli cuts, thawed, may be substituted.

In small bowl, combine steak sauce, soy sauce and garlic. Pour marinade over steak in nonmetal dish. Cover; refrigerate 1 hour, stirring occasionally.

Remove steak from marinade; reserve marinade. In large lightly oiled skillet, over medium-high heat, stir-fry steak 3 to 4 minutes or until steak is no longer pink. Remove steak with slotted spoon; keep warm.

In same skillet, heat vegetables and reserved marinade to a boil; reduce heat to low. Cover; simmer for 2 to 3 minutes. Stir in steak. Serve over rice, if desired.
Makes 4 servings

Nutrients per serving:

Calories	209
Fat	4 g
Cholesterol	65 mg
Sodium	166 mg

Beef 'n' Broccoli

Dad's Favorite Turkey Kabobs

DAD'S FAVORITE TURKEY KABOBS

3 ears corn, cut into 1-inch pieces
2 medium zucchini, cut into ¾-inch pieces
2 red bell peppers, cut into 1-inch cubes
2 Turkey Tenderloins (about 1 pound), cut into 1-inch cubes
⅓ cup reduced-calorie Italian salad dressing
Additional reduced-calorie Italian salad dressing

In medium saucepan over high heat, blanch corn in boiling water about 1 to 2 minutes. Remove corn from saucepan and plunge into cold water.

In large glass bowl, place corn, zucchini, peppers, turkey and ⅓ cup dressing; cover and refrigerate 1 to 2 hours.

Drain turkey and vegetables, discarding marinade. Alternately thread turkey cubes and vegetables on 8 skewers, leaving ½-inch space between turkey and vegetables.

On outdoor charcoal grill, cook kabobs 18 to 20 minutes, brushing with additional dressing. Turn skewers after first 10 minutes.

Makes 4 servings, 8 kabobs

Nutrients per serving (2 kabobs):

Calories	218
Fat	4 g
Cholesterol	70 mg
Sodium	381 mg

Favorite recipe from **National Turkey Federation**

PORK SAUCED WITH MUSTARD AND GRAPES

1 cup seedless or halved, seeded Chilean grapes (red, green or combination)
6 ounces boneless pork loin, cut into ½-inch slices
1 tablespoon all-purpose flour
2 teaspoons olive oil, divided
¼ cup thinly sliced onion
1 cup low sodium chicken broth
1 tablespoon white wine vinegar
1 tablespoon brown sugar
1 tablespoon mustard
1 teaspoon mustard seeds

Rinse grapes; remove any stems and set aside. Coat pork with flour. Heat 1 teaspoon oil in large nonstick skillet over medium heat. Add pork; cook about 5 minutes, turning once. Remove; set aside. Heat remaining 1 teaspoon oil in skillet over medium-high heat; add onion. Cook and stir until onion is softened. Add ½ cup grapes and remaining ingredients. Bring to a boil; cook until reduced by half, stirring occasionally. Return pork with juices and remaining ½ cup grapes to skillet. Heat until warm.

Makes 2 servings

Nutrients per serving:	
Calories	292
Fat	8 g
Cholesterol	79 mg
Sodium	251 mg

Favorite recipe from **Chilean Fresh Fruit Association**

ITALIAN PARMESAN CHICKEN

1 cup KELLOGG'S® SPECIAL K® cereal
2 tablespoons grated Parmesan cheese
1 tablespoon all-purpose flour
2 teaspoons Italian seasoning
⅓ cup reduced calorie Italian salad dressing
4 boned, skinned chicken breasts (about 1 pound)
Vegetable cooking spray

1. In a food processor or electric blender container, process Kellogg's® Special K® cereal, Parmesan cheese, flour and Italian seasoning until cereal resembles fine crumbs. Place mixture in shallow bowl; set aside.

2. Pour salad dressing into another shallow bowl. Dip chicken in salad dressing. Coat with cereal mixture. Place in single layer in shallow baking pan coated with cooking spray.

3. Bake at 350°F about 30 minutes or until tender. Do not cover or turn chicken while baking.

Makes 4 servings

Nutrients per serving:	
Calories	230
Fat	6 g
Cholesterol	70 mg
Sodium	485 mg

POLLO EMPANIZADO

½ cup WISH-BONE® Italian or Robusto Italian Dressing
2 tablespoons lime juice
½ teaspoon grated lime peel
4 boneless, skinless chicken breast halves (about 1 pound), pounded ¼ inch thick
½ cup yellow cornmeal
½ teaspoon LAWRY'S® Garlic Powder with Parsley
¼ teaspoon salt
1 medium red onion, chopped
Chopped fresh coriander (cilantro) or parsley

In large, shallow baking dish, blend Italian dressing, lime juice and peel. Add chicken and turn to coat. Cover and marinate in refrigerator, turning occasionally, at least 2 hours. Meanwhile, in medium bowl, combine cornmeal, garlic powder and salt.

Remove chicken, reserving marinade. Dip chicken in cornmeal mixture, coating well. On aluminum foil-lined broiler rack or in greased shallow baking pan, arrange onion around chicken. Drizzle chicken and onion with reserved marinade. Broil, 7 minutes or until chicken is done. Sprinkle with coriander and serve with freshly ground black pepper, if desired.

Makes 4 servings

Nutrients per serving:	
Calories	261
Fat	8 g
Cholesterol	66 mg
Sodium	591 mg

BROCCOLI LASAGNA

1 tablespoon CRISCO® Vegetable Oil
1 cup chopped onion
3 cloves garlic, minced
1 can (14½ ounces) no salt added tomatoes, undrained and chopped
1 can (8 ounces) no salt added tomato sauce
1 can (6 ounces) no salt added tomato paste
1 cup thinly sliced fresh mushrooms
¼ cup chopped fresh parsley
1 tablespoon red wine vinegar
1 teaspoon dried oregano leaves
1 teaspoon dried basil leaves
1 bay leaf
½ teaspoon salt
¼ teaspoon crushed red pepper
1½ cups lowfat cottage cheese
1 cup (4 ounces) shredded low moisture part-skim mozzarella cheese, divided
6 lasagna noodles, cooked (without salt or fat) and well drained
3 cups chopped broccoli, cooked and well drained
1 tablespoon grated Parmesan cheese

1. Heat oven to 350°F. Oil 11¾×7½×2-inch baking dish lightly.

2. Heat 1 tablespoon Crisco Oil in large saucepan on medium heat. Add onion and garlic. Cook and stir until tender. Stir in tomatoes, tomato sauce, tomato paste, mushrooms, parsley, vinegar, oregano, basil, bay leaf, salt and crushed red pepper. Bring to a boil. Reduce heat to low. Cover. Simmer 30 minutes, stirring occasionally. Remove bay leaf.

3. Combine cottage cheese and ½ cup mozzarella cheese in small bowl. Stir well.

4. Place 2 lasagna noodles in bottom of baking dish. Layer with 1 cup broccoli, one-third of the tomato sauce and one-third of the cottage cheese mixture. Repeat layers. Cover with foil.

5. Bake at 350°F for 25 minutes. Uncover. Sprinkle with remaining ½ cup mozzarella cheese and Parmesan cheese. Bake, uncovered, 10 minutes or until cheese melts. Let stand 10 minutes before serving.

Makes 8 servings

Nutrients per serving (one-eighth of recipe):

Calories	195
Fat	6 g
Cholesterol	10 mg
Sodium	440 mg

Broccoli Lasagna

TOMATO, BASIL & BROCCOLI CHICKEN

- **4 skinless, boneless chicken breast halves**
- **Salt and pepper (optional)**
- **2 tablespoons margarine or butter**
- **1 package (6.9 ounces) RICE-A-RONI® Chicken Flavor**
- **1 teaspoon dried basil leaves**
- **2 cups broccoli flowerets**
- **1 medium tomato, seeded, chopped**
- **1 cup (4 ounces) shredded mozzarella cheese**

1. Sprinkle chicken with salt and pepper, if desired.

2. In large skillet, melt margarine over medium-high heat. Add chicken; cook 2 minutes on each side or until browned. Remove from skillet; set aside, reserving drippings. Keep warm.

3. In same skillet, sauté rice-vermicelli mix in reserved drippings over medium heat until vermicelli is golden brown. Stir in 2½ cups water, contents of seasoning packet and basil. Place chicken over rice mixture; bring to a boil over high heat.

4. Cover; reduce heat. Simmer 15 minutes. Top with broccoli and tomato.

5. Cover; continue to simmer 5 minutes or until liquid is absorbed and chicken is no longer pink in center. Sprinkle with cheese. Cover; let stand a few minutes before serving.

Makes 4 servings

Nutrients per serving:	
Calories	460
Fat	14 g
Cholesterol	90 mg
Sodium	975 mg

Tomato, Basil & Broccoli Chicken

SPECTACULAR SIDES

ALMOND BROWN RICE STUFFING

⅓ cup slivered almonds
2 teaspoons margarine
2 medium tart apples, cored and diced
½ cup chopped onion
½ cup chopped celery
½ teaspoon poultry seasoning
¼ teaspoon dried thyme leaves
¼ teaspoon ground white pepper
3 cups cooked brown rice (cooked in chicken broth)

Cook almonds in margarine in large skillet over medium-high heat until browned. Add apples, onion, celery, poultry seasoning, thyme, and pepper; cook until vegetables are tender-crisp. Stir in rice; cook until thoroughly heated. Serve or use as stuffing for poultry or pork roast. Stuffing may be baked in covered baking dish at 375°F for 15 to 20 minutes.

Makes 6 servings

Microwave Directions: Combine almonds and margarine in 2- to 3-quart microproof baking dish. Cook on HIGH (100% power) 2 to 3 minutes or until browned. Add apples, onion, celery, poultry seasoning, thyme, and pepper. Cover with waxed paper and cook on HIGH 2 minutes. Stir in rice; cook on HIGH 2 to 3 minutes, stirring after 1½ minutes, or until thoroughly heated. Serve as above.

Variations: *For Mushroom Stuffing, add 2 cups (about 8 ounces) sliced mushrooms; cook with apples, onion, celery, and seasonings. For Raisin Stuffing, add ½ cup raisins; cook with apples, onion, celery, and seasonings.*

Nutrients per serving:	
Calories	198
Fat	6 g
Cholesterol	0 mg
Sodium	30 mg

Favorite recipe from **USA Rice Council**

Almond Brown Rice Stuffing

Dilled New Potatoes and Peas

DILLED NEW POTATOES AND PEAS

1 pound (6 to 8) small new potatoes, quartered
2 cups frozen peas
1 jar (12 ounces) HEINZ® HomeStyle Turkey Gravy
½ cup light dairy sour cream
1 teaspoon dried dill weed

Cook potatoes in 2-quart saucepan in lightly salted boiling water 10 to 15 minutes or until tender. Add peas; cook 1 minute. Drain well. Combine gravy, sour cream and dill; stir into vegetable mixture. Heat (do not boil), stirring occasionally.

Makes 8 servings, about 4 cups

Microwave Directions: Place potatoes and 2 tablespoons water in 2-quart casserole. Cover with lid or vented plastic wrap. Microwave at HIGH (100%) 6 to 7 minutes or until potatoes are just tender, stirring once. Stir in peas. Cover and microwave at HIGH 1 minute. Combine gravy, sour cream and dill; stir into vegetable mixture. Cover and microwave at HIGH 7 to 8 minutes or until heated through, stirring once.

Nutrients per serving (about ½ cup):

Calories	126
Fat	1 g
Cholesterol	6 mg
Sodium	332 mg

RISOTTO MILANESE

1 small onion, thinly sliced
1 tablespoon margarine
1 cup uncooked arborio or other short-grain rice
Pinch saffron
½ cup dry white wine
¼ teaspoon TABASCO® pepper sauce
2 cups low sodium chicken broth, divided
Hot water
¼ cup grated Parmesan cheese
Salt and freshly ground white pepper (optional)

In large skillet, cook and stir onion in margarine over medium-high heat until soft. Add rice and saffron; stir constantly 2 to 3 minutes. Add wine and TABASCO sauce; stir until absorbed. Stir in 1 cup broth. Cook, uncovered, stirring frequently until broth is absorbed. Add remaining broth and hot water, ½ cup at a time, stirring constantly from bottom and side of pan. (Wait until rice just begins to dry out before adding more liquid.) Continue stirring and adding water until rice is tender but firm to the bite and has the consistency of creamy rice pudding. (The total amount of liquid used will vary. Watch rice carefully to ensure proper consistency.) Stir in cheese and salt and pepper, if desired.

Makes 6 servings

Nutrients per serving:

Calories	178
Fat	4 g
Cholesterol	3 mg
Sodium	94 mg

TOMATOES WITH BASIL CREAM

1 clove garlic
1 container (8 ounces) ⅓ less fat PHILADELPHIA BRAND® Pasteurized Process Cream Cheese Product
2 tablespoons white wine vinegar
2 tablespoons chopped fresh basil
2 tablespoons chopped fresh parsley, divided
½ teaspoon salt
¼ teaspoon black pepper
2 red tomatoes, thinly sliced
2 yellow tomatoes, thinly sliced

Place garlic in blender or food processor container; cover. Process until finely chopped.

Add cream cheese product, vinegar, basil, 1 tablespoon parsley, salt and pepper; blend until smooth.

Arrange tomatoes on serving platter. Spoon cream cheese mixture over tomatoes. Sprinkle with remaining 1 tablespoon parsley. Garnish with fresh basil leaves, if desired.

Makes 10 servings

Prep Time: 15 minutes

Nutrients per serving:

Calories	60
Fat	trace
Cholesterol	15 mg
Sodium	240 mg

CINNAMON–APPLE SWEET POTATOES

4 medium sweet potatoes
1½ cups finely chopped apples
½ cup orange juice
¼ cup sugar
1½ teaspoons cornstarch
½ teaspoon ground cinnamon
½ teaspoon grated orange peel

Microwave Directions: Wash sweet potatoes and prick with fork. Place on paper towels. Microwave at HIGH (100% power) 10 to 13 minutes or until tender, turning halfway through cooking. Set aside. In small bowl, combine apples, orange juice, sugar, cornstarch, cinnamon and orange peel. Cover; cook at HIGH 3 minutes. Stir mixture and continue cooking, uncovered, at HIGH 1½ to 2½ minutes or until sauce is thickened. Slit sweet potatoes and spoon sauce over each. *Makes 4 servings*

Tip: *Sauce may be made up ahead and reheated at serving time.*

Nutrients per serving:	
Calories	216
Fat	trace
Cholesterol	0 mg
Sodium	12 mg

Favorite recipe from **The Sugar Association, Inc.**

Tangy Asparagus Linguini

VEGETABLE SOUFFLÉ IN PEPPER CUPS

1 cup chopped broccoli
½ cup shredded carrot
¼ cup chopped onion
1 teaspoon dried basil leaves, crushed
½ teaspoon ground black pepper
2 teaspoons FLEISCHMANN'S® Margarine
2 tablespoons all-purpose flour
1 cup skim milk
1 cup EGG BEATERS® Healthy Real Egg Product
3 large red, green or yellow bell peppers, halved lengthwise

In nonstick skillet over medium-high heat, cook and stir broccoli, carrot, onion, basil and black pepper in margarine until vegetables are tender. Stir in flour until smooth. Gradually add milk, stirring constantly until thickened. Remove from heat; set aside.

In medium bowl, with electric mixer at high speed, beat Egg Beaters until foamy, about 3 minutes. Gently fold into broccoli mixture; spoon into bell pepper halves. Place in 13×9-inch baking pan. Bake at 375°F for 30 to 35 minutes or until knife inserted in centers comes out clean. Garnish as desired and serve immediately.

Makes 6 servings

Nutrients per serving:	
Calories	75
Fat	2 g
Cholesterol	1 mg
Sodium	91 mg

TANGY ASPARAGUS LINGUINI

2 tablespoons light margarine
¼ cup finely chopped onion
3 cloves garlic, minced
8 ounces fresh asparagus, peeled and sliced diagonally into ½-inch pieces
2 tablespoons dry white wine
2 tablespoons fresh lemon juice
Freshly ground black pepper
5 ounces linguini, cooked and drained
¼ cup (1 ounce) SARGENTO® Grated Parmesan Cheese
¾ cup (3 ounces) SARGENTO® Preferred Light® Fancy Shredded Mozzarella Cheese

Melt margarine over medium heat in large skillet. Cook and stir onion and garlic until onion is soft. Add asparagus; cook and stir an additional 2 minutes. Add wine and lemon juice; cook an additional minute. Season with pepper to taste. Remove from heat. In large bowl, toss hot pasta, Parmesan cheese and asparagus mixture. Remove to serving platter; sprinkle with mozzarella cheese. Garnish, if desired. Serve immediately. *Makes 4 servings*

Nutrients per serving:	
Calories	254
Fat	8 g
Cholesterol	13 mg
Sodium	317 mg

APPLE STUFFING

1 cup finely chopped onion
½ cup finely chopped celery
½ cup unpeeled, finely chopped apple
1½ cups MOTT'S® Natural Apple Sauce
1 (8-ounce) package stuffing mix (original or cornbread)
1 cup low-fat reduced-sodium chicken broth
1½ teaspoons dried thyme leaves
1 teaspoon ground sage
½ teaspoon salt
½ teaspoon black pepper

1. Spray medium nonstick skillet with nonstick cooking spray. Heat over medium heat until hot. Add onion and celery; cook and stir about 5 minutes or until transparent. Add apple; cook and stir about 3 minutes or until golden. Transfer to large bowl. Stir in apple sauce, stuffing mix, broth, thyme, sage, salt and black pepper.

2. Loosely stuff chicken or turkey just before roasting or place stuffing in greased 8-inch square pan. Cover pan; bake in preheated 350°F oven 20 to 25 minutes or until hot. Refrigerate leftovers.
Makes 8 servings

Note: Cooked stuffing can also be used to fill centers of cooked acorn squash.

Nutrients per serving:	
Calories	150
Fat	2 g
Cholesterol	0 mg
Sodium	620 mg

NOT FRIED ASIAN RICE

2 teaspoons sesame oil
¾ cup chopped green onions
½ cup chopped red bell pepper
2 cloves garlic, minced
2 cups water
1 cup uncooked converted rice
2 egg whites
1 tablespoon light soy sauce
2 teaspoons sugar

Heat oil in nonstick skillet over medium-high heat until hot. Add onions, bell pepper and garlic; cook and stir 1 minute. Add water and bring to a boil. Reduce heat to low; stir in rice and egg whites. Simmer 20 minutes or until rice is tender, stirring frequently. Stir in soy sauce and sugar. Cook 3 to 5 minutes more until sugar caramelizes. *Makes 6 servings*

Nutrients per serving:	
Calories	145
Fat	2 g
Cholesterol	0 mg
Sodium	108 mg

Favorite recipe from **The Sugar Association, Inc.**

Apple Stuffing

Couscous with Summer Vegetables

1½ cups PRITIKIN® Chicken Broth or water
1 cup whole wheat couscous
1 large onion, chopped
1 medium red bell pepper, diced
1 small yellow squash or zucchini, sliced
2 cloves garlic, minced
1 medium tomato, seeded and chopped
¼ cup chopped fresh basil

Bring broth to a boil in small saucepan. Stir in couscous; reduce heat to low. Cover and simmer 5 minutes or until most of liquid is absorbed. Meanwhile, lightly spray large skillet with nonstick cooking spray. Add onion, bell pepper, squash and garlic. Cook over medium-high heat 5 minutes or until vegetables are tender, stirring frequently. Add cooked couscous, tomato and basil; heat through. Serve with freshly ground black pepper, if desired.

Makes 6 servings

Nutrients per serving:

Calories	140
Fat	0 g
Cholesterol	0 mg
Sodium	110 mg

Couscous with Summer Vegetables

CRISPENED NEW POTATOES

1½ pounds new potatoes (about 12)
½ cup QUAKER® Oat Bran hot cereal, uncooked
2 tablespoons grated Parmesan cheese
1 tablespoon snipped fresh parsley *or* 1 teaspoon dried parsley flakes
½ teaspoon snipped fresh dill *or* ½ teaspoon dried dill weed
½ teaspoon paprika
1 egg white, slightly beaten
¼ cup skim milk
1 tablespoon margarine, melted

Heat oven to 400°F. Lightly spray 11×7-inch dish with nonstick cooking spray or oil lightly. Cook whole potatoes in boiling water 15 minutes. Drain; rinse in cold water.

In shallow dish, combine oat bran, cheese, parsley, dill and paprika. In another shallow dish, combine egg white and milk. Coat each potato in oat bran mixture; shake off excess. Dip into egg mixture, then coat again with oat bran mixture. Place in prepared dish; drizzle with margarine. Cover; bake 10 minutes. Uncover; bake an additional 10 minutes or until potatoes are tender.

Makes 4 servings

Nutrients per serving:	
Calories	230
Fat	5 g
Cholesterol	0 mg
Sodium	110 mg

SWEET AND SOUR RED CABBAGE

1 small head red cabbage (1 pound), shredded
1 medium apple, unpeeled, cored, shredded
1 small potato, peeled, shredded
1 small onion, chopped
Grated peel of ½ SUNKIST® Lemon
Juice of 1 SUNKIST® Lemon
3 tablespoons firmly packed brown sugar
1 tablespoon red wine vinegar

In large, covered nonstick skillet, cook cabbage, apple, potato and onion in 1 cup water over low heat for 15 minutes; stir occasionally. Add lemon peel, lemon juice, brown sugar and vinegar. Cover; cook over low heat an additional 10 minutes, stirring often, until vegetables are tender and mixture thickens slightly.

Makes 6 servings

Nutrients per serving (¾ cup):	
Calories	74
Fat	0 g
Cholesterol	0 mg
Sodium	11 mg

APRICOT-GLAZED BEETS

1 large bunch fresh beets *or* 1 pound loose beets
1 cup apricot nectar
1 tablespoon cornstarch
2 tablespoons cider or red wine vinegar
8 dried apricot halves, cut into strips
¼ teaspoon salt
Additional apricot halves (optional)

Cut tops off beets, leaving at least 1 inch of stems (do not trim root ends). Scrub beets under running water with soft vegetable brush, being careful not to break skins. Place beets in medium saucepan; cover with water. Cover. Bring to a boil over high heat; reduce heat to medium. Simmer beets about 20 minutes or until just barely firm when pierced with fork and skins rub off easily. (Larger beets will take longer to cook.) Transfer to plate; cool. Rinse pan.

Combine apricot nectar and cornstarch in same saucepan; stir in vinegar. Add apricot strips and salt. Cook over medium heat until mixture thickens.

Cut roots and stems from beets on plate.* Peel, halve and cut beets into ¼-inch-thick slices. Add beet slices to apricot mixture; toss gently to coat. Transfer to warm serving dish. Garnish as desired. Serve immediately with apricot halves.

Makes 4 side-dish servings

*Do not cut beets on cutting board; the juice will stain the board.

Nutrients per serving:	
Calories	93
Fat	trace
Cholesterol	0 mg
Sodium	175 mg

VEGETABLE OAT PILAF

½ cup chopped mushrooms
½ cup chopped green bell pepper
½ cup sliced green onions
1 tablespoon vegetable oil
1¾ cups QUAKER® Oats (quick or old fashioned, uncooked)
2 egg whites *or* ¼ cup egg substitute
¾ cup low-sodium chicken broth
1 medium tomato, seeded, chopped

In large saucepan, cook and stir mushrooms, green pepper and onions in oil over medium heat 2 to 3 minutes. In small bowl, mix oats and egg whites until oats are evenly coated. Add oats to vegetable mixture in saucepan; cook and stir over medium heat until oats are dry and separated, about 5 to 6 minutes. Add broth; continue cooking and stirring 2 to 3 minutes until liquid is absorbed. Stir in tomato. Serve immediately.

Makes 8 servings

Nutrients per serving:	
Calories	101
Fat	3 g
Cholesterol	0 mg
Sodium	20 mg

Apricot-Glazed Beets

Zucchini Bake

⅔ cup QUAKER® Oat Bran hot cereal, uncooked
½ teaspoon Italian seasoning
¼ teaspoon black pepper
1 egg white
1 tablespoon water
2 medium zucchini, sliced ¾ inch thick, quartered (about 3 cups)
1 small onion, chopped
⅔ cup low-sodium tomato sauce
2 teaspoons olive oil
2 teaspoons grated Parmesan cheese
¼ cup (1 ounce) shredded part-skim mozzarella cheese

Heat oven to 375°F. Lightly spray 8-inch square baking dish with nonstick cooking spray, or oil lightly. In large plastic food bag, combine oat bran, Italian seasoning and pepper; mix well. In shallow dish, lightly beat egg white and water. Coat zucchini with oat bran mixture; shake off excess. Dip into egg mixture, then coat again with oat bran mixture. Place zucchini in prepared dish; sprinkle with onion. Spoon combined tomato sauce and oil over vegetables. Sprinkle with Parmesan cheese. Bake 30 minutes or until zucchini is crisp-tender; top with mozzarella cheese. Serve warm.

Makes 9 servings

Microwave Directions: In large plastic food bag, combine oat bran, Italian seasoning and pepper; mix well. In shallow dish, lightly beat egg white and water. Coat zucchini with oat bran mixture; shake off excess. Dip into egg mixture, then coat again with oat bran mixture. Place zucchini in 8-inch square microwavable dish; sprinkle with onion. Spoon combined tomato sauce and oil over vegetables. Sprinkle with Parmesan cheese. Microwave at HIGH (100% power) 5½ to 6½ minutes or until zucchini is crisp-tender, rotating dish ½ turn after 3 minutes. Sprinkle with mozzarella cheese. Let stand 3 minutes before serving. Serve warm.

Nutrients per serving:	
Calories	60
Fat	2 g
Cholesterol	1 mg
Sodium	35 mg

Shrimp Stuffing

1 pound raw shrimp, cleaned, quartered
2 tablespoons margarine
1 package (6 ounces) KELLOGG'S® CROUTETTES® Stuffing Mix
½ cup chopped celery
½ cup sliced green onions
¼ cup chopped green pepper
1 can (10¾ ounces) condensed cream of mushroom soup
¾ cup water
1 teaspoon dry mustard
1 teaspoon lemon juice
½ teaspoon Cajun seasoning
¼ teaspoon salt (optional)
½ cup (2 ounces) shredded part-skim mozzarella cheese

Shrimp Stuffing

In 12-inch skillet, cook shrimp in margarine over medium heat just until shrimp start to change color.

Stir in stuffing mix, celery, green onions, green pepper, soup, water, mustard, lemon juice, seasoning and salt, tossing gently to moisten. Reduce heat to low. Cover and cook 5 minutes. Remove from heat and stir in cheese.

Makes 8 servings

Microwave Directions: Combine shrimp and margarine in 4-quart microwave-safe mixing bowl. Microwave at HIGH (100%) 1 minute. Stir in stuffing mix, celery, green onions, green pepper, soup, water, mustard, lemon juice, seasoning and salt. Cover with plastic wrap, leaving a corner open as a vent. Microwave at HIGH 9 minutes or until stuffing is hot and shrimp are cooked, stirring every 3 minutes. (When stirring stuffing, carefully remove plastic from bowl to allow steam to escape.) Stir in cheese.

Nutrients per serving:

Calories	220
Fat	7 g
Cholesterol	95 mg
Sodium	827 mg

SWEET TREATS

CHOCOLATE AND RASPBERRY CREAM TORTE

6 tablespoons extra light corn oil spread
1 cup sugar
1 cup skim milk
1 tablespoon white vinegar
½ teaspoon vanilla extract
1¼ cups all-purpose flour
⅓ cup HERSHEY®S Cocoa or HERSHEY®S European Style Cocoa
1 teaspoon baking soda
¼ cup red raspberry jam
Raspberry Cream (recipe follows)

Heat oven to 350°F. Spray 15½×10½×1-inch jelly-roll pan with vegetable cooking spray. In medium saucepan over low heat, melt corn oil spread; stir in sugar. Remove from heat; stir in milk, vinegar and vanilla. In small bowl, stir together flour, cocoa and baking soda; add gradually to sugar mixture, stirring with whisk until well blended. Pour into prepared pan.

Bake 16 to 18 minutes or until wooden pick inserted in center comes out clean. Cool 10 minutes; remove from pan to wire rack. Cool completely. To assemble, cut cake crosswise into four pieces. Place one piece on serving plate; spread 1 tablespoon jam over top. Carefully spread a scant ¾ cup Raspberry Cream over jam. Repeat procedure with remaining cake layers, jam and Raspberry Cream, ending with plain layer on top. Spread remaining 1 tablespoon jam over top. Spoon or pipe remaining Raspberry Cream over jam. Refrigerate torte until ready to serve. Garnish as desired. Cover; refrigerate leftover torte.

Makes 14 servings

Raspberry Cream: Thaw and thoroughly drain 1 package (10 ounces) frozen red raspberries. In blender container, place raspberries. Cover; blend until smooth. Strain in sieve; discard seeds. In small mixer bowl, prepare 1 envelope (1.3 ounces) dry whipped topping mix as directed on package, using ½ cup cold skim milk, omitting vanilla and adding 2 to 3 drops red food color, if desired. Fold in puréed raspberries.

Nutrients per serving:

Calories	170
Fat	3 g
Cholesterol	0 mg
Sodium	100 mg

Chocolate and Raspberry Cream Torte

Choco–Lowfat Strawberry Shortbread Bars

¼ cup (½ stick) light corn oil spread
½ cup sugar
1 egg white
1¼ cups all-purpose flour
¼ cup HERSHEY®S Cocoa or HERSHEY®S European Style Cocoa
¾ teaspoon cream of tartar
½ teaspoon baking soda
Dash salt
½ cup strawberry all-fruit spread
Vanilla Chip Drizzle (recipe follows)

Heat oven to 375°F. Lightly spray 13×9×2-inch baking pan with vegetable cooking spray. In mixer bowl, combine corn oil spread and sugar; beat on medium speed of electric mixer until well blended. Add egg white; beat until well blended. In small bowl, stir together flour, cocoa, cream of tartar, baking soda and salt; beat gradually into sugar mixture. Gently press mixture onto bottom of prepared pan.

Bake 10 to 12 minutes or just until set. Cool completely in pan on wire rack. Spread fruit spread evenly over crust. Cut into bars or other desired shapes with small cookie cutters. Drizzle Vanilla Chip Drizzle over tops of bars. Let stand until set. Store, covered, at room temperature.

Makes 3 dozen bars

Vanilla Chip Drizzle: In small microwave-safe bowl, place ⅓ cup HERSHEY®S Vanilla Milk Chips and ½ teaspoon shortening (do not use butter, margarine or oil). Microwave at HIGH (100%) 30 seconds; stir vigorously. If necessary, microwave at HIGH an additional 15 seconds until chips are melted and mixture is smooth when stirred. Use immediately.

Nutrients per serving:	
Calories	50
Fat	1 g
Cholesterol	0 mg
Sodium	45 mg

Fruit Lover's Tart

1¼ cups QUAKER® Oats (quick or old fashioned, uncooked)
⅓ cup firmly packed brown sugar
¼ cup all-purpose flour
2 tablespoons margarine, melted
2 egg whites
1 cup (8 ounces) part-skim ricotta cheese
¼ cup (2 ounces) Neufchâtel cheese, softened
2 tablespoons powdered sugar
½ teaspoon grated lemon peel
4½ cups any combination sliced fresh or frozen fruit, thawed, well drained

Heat oven to 350°F. Lightly spray 9-inch pie plate with nonstick cooking spray, or oil lightly. Combine oats, brown sugar, flour, margarine and egg whites, mixing until moistened. Press mixture onto bottom and up side of prepared plate. Bake 15 to 18 minutes or until light golden brown. Remove to wire rack; cool completely. Combine cheeses, powdered sugar and lemon peel. Spread onto oat base; top with fruit. Refrigerate 2 hours.

Microwave Directions: Combine oats, brown sugar, flour, margarine and egg whites, mixing until moistened. Press mixture onto bottom and up side of 9-inch microwavable pie plate. Microwave on HIGH (100% power) 2½ to 3 minutes or until top springs back when lightly touched. Cool completely. Proceed as directed.

Makes 1 (9-inch) pie, 8 servings

Nutrients per serving:	
Calories	240
Fat	8 g
Cholesterol	15 mg
Sodium	110 mg

Fruit Lover's Tart

Baked Apple Crisp

BAKED APPLE CRISP

- **8 cups unpeeled, thinly sliced apples (about 8 medium)**
- **2 tablespoons granulated sugar**
- **4½ teaspoons lemon juice**
- **4 teaspoons ground cinnamon, divided**
- **1½ cups MOTT'S® Natural Apple Sauce**
- **1 cup uncooked rolled oats**
- **½ cup firmly packed light brown sugar**
- **⅓ cup all-purpose flour**
- **⅓ cup evaporated skim milk**
- **¼ cup nonfat dry milk powder**
- **1 cup vanilla nonfat yogurt**

1. Preheat oven to 350°F. Spray 2-quart casserole dish with nonstick cooking spray.

2. In large bowl, toss apple slices with granulated sugar, lemon juice and 2 teaspoons cinnamon. Spoon into prepared dish. Spread apple sauce evenly over apple mixture.

3. In medium bowl, combine oats, brown sugar, flour, evaporated milk, dry milk powder and remaining 2 teaspoons cinnamon. Spread over apple sauce.

4. Bake 35 to 40 minutes or until lightly browned and bubbly. Cool slightly; serve warm. Top each serving with dollop of yogurt.

Makes 12 servings

Nutrients per serving:	
Calories	185
Fat	2 g
Cholesterol	0 mg
Sodium	35 mg

ORANGE–ALMOND ANGEL FOOD CAKE

1 cup whole natural California Almonds
1 package (14.5 ounces) angel food cake mix, plus ingredients to prepare mix
1⅓ cups orange juice
2 tablespoons grated orange peel
Sorbet (optional)
Fresh fruit (optional)

Preheat oven to 350°F. Spread almonds in single layer on baking sheet. Toast in oven 12 to 15 minutes until lightly browned, stirring occasionally; cool and chop.

Prepare cake mix according to package directions, substituting orange juice for water called for in package directions. Fold in grated orange peel and ½ cup chopped almonds. Spoon batter into ungreased 10-inch tube pan. Sprinkle with remaining chopped almonds. Bake and cool according to package directions. Serve with sorbet and fresh fruit, if desired.

Makes 10 servings

Nutrients per serving:	
Calories	271
Fat	8 g
Cholesterol	0 mg
Sodium	181 mg

Favorite recipe from **Almond Board of California**

ICED COFFEE AND CHOCOLATE PIE

2 envelopes unflavored gelatin
¼ cup cold skim milk
1 cup skim milk, heated to boiling
2 cups vanilla ice milk
⅓ cup sugar
2 tablespoons instant coffee granules
1 teaspoon vanilla extract
1 (6-ounce) KEEBLER® READY–CRUST® Chocolate Flavored Pie Crust
Reduced-calorie whipped topping (optional)
Chocolate curls (optional)

In blender container, sprinkle gelatin over ¼ cup cold milk; mix on low. Let stand 3 to 4 minutes to soften. Add hot milk; cover and mix on low until gelatin dissolves, about 2 minutes. Add ice milk, sugar, coffee granules and vanilla. Cover and mix until smooth. Pour into KEEBLER® READY–CRUST®.

Refrigerate at least 2 hours. Garnish with whipped topping and chocolate curls, if desired.

Makes 1 pie, 8 servings

Nutrients per serving:	
Calories	220
Fat	6 g
Cholesterol	6 mg
Sodium	210 mg

NO-BAKE PINEAPPLE MARMALADE SQUARES

1 cup graham cracker crumbs
½ cup plus 2 tablespoons sugar, divided
¼ cup light margarine, melted
1 cup fat free or light sour cream
4 ounces light cream cheese, softened
¼ cup orange marmalade or apricot fruit spread, divided
1 can (20 ounces) DOLE® Crushed Pineapple
1 envelope unflavored gelatin

• **Combine** graham cracker crumbs, 2 tablespoons sugar and margarine in 8-inch square glass baking dish; pat mixture firmly and evenly onto bottom of dish. Freeze 10 minutes.

• **Beat** sour cream, cream cheese, remaining ½ cup sugar and 1 tablespoon marmalade in medium bowl until smooth and blended; set aside.

• **Drain** pineapple; reserve ¼ cup juice.

• **Sprinkle** gelatin over reserved juice in small saucepan; let stand 1 minute. Cook and stir over low heat until gelatin dissolves.

• **Beat** gelatin mixture into sour cream mixture until well blended. Spoon mixture evenly over crust.

• **Stir** together pineapple and remaining 3 tablespoons marmalade in small bowl until blended. Evenly spoon over sour cream filling. Cover and refrigerate 2 hours or until firm.

Makes 16 servings

Nutrients per serving:

Calories	220
Fat	6 g
Cholesterol	4 mg
Sodium	181 mg

No-Bake Pineapple Marmalade Squares

THREE–BERRY KUCHEN

- 1¾ cups all-purpose flour, divided
- 2 teaspoons baking powder
- ½ teaspoon baking soda
- ½ teaspoon salt
- ⅔ cup MOTT'S® Apple Sauce
- 4 egg whites
- ¼ cup plain nonfat yogurt
- 2 tablespoons granulated sugar
- 1 teaspoon grated lemon peel
- 2 cups assorted fresh or thawed frozen blueberries, raspberries or blackberries
- ¼ cup firmly packed light brown sugar
- 2 tablespoons margarine

1. Preheat oven to 350°F. Spray 10-inch round cake pan with nonstick cooking spray.

2. In small bowl, combine 1½ cups flour, baking powder, baking soda and salt.

3. In large bowl, whisk together apple sauce, egg whites, yogurt, granulated sugar and lemon peel.

4. Add flour mixture to apple sauce mixture; stir until well blended. Spread batter into prepared pan.

5. Sprinkle berries over batter. Combine remaining ¼ cup flour and brown sugar in small bowl. Cut in margarine with pastry blender or fork until mixture resembles coarse crumbs. Sprinkle over berries.

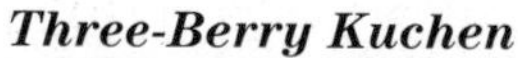

Three-Berry Kuchen

6. Bake 50 to 55 minutes or until lightly browned. Cool on wire rack 20 minutes. Serve warm or cool completely. Cut into 9 slices.

Makes 9 servings

Nutrients per serving:

Calories	190
Fat	3 g
Cholesterol	0 mg
Sodium	290 mg

COCOA BANANA BARS

BARS

- **⅔ cup QUAKER® Oat Bran hot cereal, uncooked**
- **⅔ cup all-purpose flour**
- **½ cup granulated sugar**
- **⅓ cup unsweetened cocoa**
- **½ cup mashed ripe banana (about 1 large)**
- **¼ cup liquid vegetable oil margarine**
- **3 tablespoons light corn syrup**
- **2 egg whites, slightly beaten**
- **1 teaspoon vanilla**

GLAZE

- **2 teaspoons unsweetened cocoa**
- **2 teaspoons liquid vegetable oil margarine**
- **¼ cup powdered sugar**
- **2 to 2½ teaspoons warm water, divided**
- **Strawberry halves (optional)**

For Bars, heat oven to 350°F. Lightly spray 8-inch square baking pan with nonstick cooking spray, or oil lightly. In large bowl, combine oat bran, flour, granulated sugar and ⅓ cup cocoa. Add combined banana, ¼ cup margarine, corn syrup, egg whites and vanilla; mix well. Pour into prepared pan, spreading evenly. Bake 23 to 25 minutes or until center is set. Cool on wire rack. Drizzle Glaze over brownies. Top with strawberry halves, if desired. Cut into bars. Store tightly covered.

For Glaze, in small bowl combine 2 teaspoons cocoa and 2 teaspoons margarine. Stir in powdered sugar and 1 teaspoon of the water. Gradually add remaining 1 to 1½ teaspoons water to make medium-thick glaze, mixing well.

Makes 9 bar cookies

Nutrients per serving (1 bar):

Calories	210
Fat	7 g
Cholesterol	0 mg
Sodium	60 mg

Hershey®s Slimmed Down Chocolate Cake

HERSHEY®S SLIMMED DOWN CHOCOLATE CAKE

- **1¼ cups all-purpose flour**
- **⅓ cup HERSHEY®S Cocoa**
- **1 teaspoon baking soda**
- **6 tablespoons extra light corn oil spread**
- **1 cup sugar**
- **1 cup skim milk**
- **1 tablespoon white vinegar**
- **½ teaspoon vanilla extract**
- **Slimmed Down Cocoa Frosting or Slimmed Down Cocoa Almond Frosting (recipes follow)**

Heat oven to 350°F. Spray two 8-inch round baking pans with vegetable cooking spray. In small bowl, stir together flour, cocoa and baking soda. In medium saucepan over low heat, melt corn oil spread; stir in sugar. Remove from heat. Add milk, vinegar and vanilla to mixture in saucepan; stir. Add flour mixture; stir with whisk until well blended. Pour batter into prepared pans.

Bake 20 minutes or until wooden pick inserted in centers comes out clean. Cool 10 minutes; remove from pans to wire racks. Cool completely. To assemble, place one cake layer on serving plate; spread half of frosting over top. Set second cake layer on top; spread remaining frosting over top. Refrigerate 2 to 3 hours or until chilled before serving. Garnish as desired. Cover; refrigerate leftover cake.

Makes 12 servings

Slimmed Down Cocoa Frosting: In small mixer bowl, stir together 1 envelope (1.3 ounces) dry whipped topping mix, ½ cup cold skim milk, 1 tablespoon HERSHEY'®S Cocoa and ½ teaspoon vanilla extract. Beat on high speed of electric mixer until soft peaks form.

Slimmed Down Cocoa Almond Frosting: Prepare Slimmed Down Cocoa Frosting, substituting ¼ teaspoon almond extract for the ½ teaspoon vanilla extract.

Nutrients per serving:	
Calories	160
Fat	4 g
Cholesterol	0 mg
Sodium	115 mg

PINEAPPLE UPSIDE DOWN CAKE

2 cans (8 ounces each) pineapple slices in juice, undrained
¼ cup raisins
1 cup KELLOGG'S® ALL–BRAN® cereal
¾ cup whole wheat flour
½ cup all-purpose flour
1 teaspoon baking soda
1 teaspoon ground cinnamon
¼ teaspoon salt (optional)
3 tablespoons margarine, softened
¼ cup sugar
4 egg whites
1 cup (8 ounces) vanilla-flavored low-fat yogurt
1 teaspoon vanilla extract

Drain pineapple, reserving ¼ cup juice. Arrange pineapple slices in 9-inch round cake pan coated with nonstick cooking spray. Place raisins around and in centers of pineapple slices.

Stir together Kellogg's® All-Bran® cereal, whole wheat flour, all-purpose flour, baking soda, cinnamon and salt. Set aside.

In large mixing bowl, beat together margarine and sugar. Add egg whites, yogurt, vanilla and ¼ cup reserved pineapple juice, mixing until blended. Add flour mixture, stirring only until combined. Spread batter over pineapple slices and raisins.

Bake at 350°F about 35 minutes or until wooden toothpick inserted in center comes out clean. Let stand 10 minutes. Turn cake upside down onto serving plate. Remove pan. Cool. Cut into 12 wedges.

Makes 12 servings

Nutrients per serving:	
Calories	150
Fat	3 g
Cholesterol	0 mg
Sodium	240 mg

Blueberry Angel Food Cake Rolls

BLUEBERRY ANGEL FOOD CAKE ROLLS

1 package DUNCAN HINES® Angel Food Cake Mix
Confectioners sugar
1 can (21 ounces) blueberry pie filling
¼ cup confectioners sugar
Mint leaves, for garnish (optional)

1. Preheat oven to 350°F. Line two 15½×10½×1-inch jelly-roll pans with aluminum foil.

2. Prepare cake following package directions. Divide into pans. Spread evenly. Cut through batter with knife or spatula to remove large air bubbles. Bake at 350°F for 15 minutes or until set. Invert cakes at once onto clean, lint-free dishtowels dusted with confectioners sugar. Remove foil carefully. Roll up each cake with towel jelly-roll fashion, starting at short end. Cool completely.

3. Unroll cakes. Spread about 1 cup blueberry pie filling to within 1 inch of edges on each cake. Reroll and place seam-side down on serving plate. Dust with ¼ cup confectioners sugar. Garnish with mint leaves, if desired.

Makes 2 cakes, 8 servings each

Nutrients per serving:

Calories	143
Fat	0 g
Cholesterol	0 mg
Sodium	77 mg

ACKNOWLEDGMENTS

The publishers would like to thank the companies and organizations listed below for the use of their recipes and photographs in this publication.

Almond Board of California
California Tree Fruit Agreement
Chilean Fresh Fruit Association
Del Monte Foods
Dole Food Company, Inc.
Florida Tomato Committee
Golden Grain/Mission Pasta
Heinz U.S.A.
Hershey Foods Corporation
Keebler® Company
Kellogg Company
Kraft Foods, Inc.
Thomas J. Liption Co.
McIlhenny Company
MOTTS® Inc., a division of Cadbury Beverages Inc.
Nabisco, Inc.
National Pork Producers Council
National Turkey Federation
Nestlé Food Company
Perdue® Farms
The Procter & Gamble Company
The Quaker Oats Company
Ralston Foods, Inc,
Sargento Foods Inc.®
Sunkist Growers
Surimi Seafood Education Center
The Sugar Association, Inc.
USA Rice Council
Wisconsin Milk Marketing Board

INDEX